D1557578

STEVE:

I HOPE YOU ENJOY THIS.....(AND OF COURSE,
TELL ALL YOUR READERS TO BUY ONE)

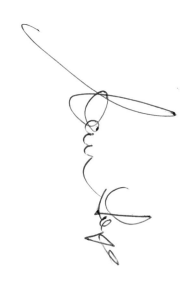

A KICK IN THE GRASS

Clive Toye

S J P

ST. JOHANN PRESS
HAWORTH, NJ

ST. JOHANN PRESS

Published in the United States of America
by St. Johann Press
P.O. Box 241
Haworth, NJ 07641

Library of Congress Cataloging-in-Publication Data

Data pending

The paper used in this publication meets the minimum requirements of the American
National Standard for Information Sciences—Permanence of Paper for Printed Library
Materials, ANSI/NISO Z39/48–1992

Designed, typeset, printed and bound in the United States

by G&H Soho, Inc.
117 Grand Street
Hoboken, NJ 07030
www.ghsoho.com

Dedicated to my father, Chief Petty Officer T R Toye
Who taught me love of soccer, pride in service
and how to be a good father

And to my mother, Irene Toye
Who taught me how to be determined, self-reliant
and so much, much more

CONTENTS

PROLOGUE

AMERICANS AND HISTORY are not easy partners.

The US of A is still a country thrusting forward, reinvigorated with each generation and with a constant inflow of immigrants whose memories are elsewhere. I was never so conscious of this as one day in Miami, strolling up towards the new, modern bustling Bayfront from the new modern Intercontinental Hotel, when I saw a stone obelisk, alone in the middle of a rubbish-strewn patch of untended grass.

So, being of curious mind, I walked over to see what it was. And what it was, begrimed, graffiti-covered and forlorn, was Miami's monument to the dead of World War II. My reaction was one of fury and then I remembered . . . remembered that Miami's population was now mostly from Cuba and Haiti and Colombia and other places where the war was unimportant, even unknown to them. Was that a reason? Or just an excuse? I don't know but it was seriously symptomatic of a frequent national attitude which, at best, is lip service to understanding what went before and, at worst, believing that nothing went before was of any importance whatsoever until I/we/my generation arrived on the scene.

Often, I think this is so with soccer in America. As I write this, soccer is still mostly ignored by the mainstream media but I can sit in New York on a weekend and watch games on TV from England, Argentina, Japan, Germany, France, Bolivia, El Salvador, Honduras, Mexico, Italy . . . more soccer in fact than anyone in any of the great soccer cities of Europe or South America.

We soccer fans do not even give it a moment's thought any more. The whole world is scoring goals in our living rooms and we take it as a matter of course. If the game we want to see isn't on Fox Soccer Channel (let me repeat that, Fox Soccer Channel, a channel devoted to soccer), it'll be on

Univision or Telemundo or MSG Network or ESPN or Gol TV. I could even see my own beloved Exeter City play Manchester United in the FA Cup and gaze at a stadium I haven't been able to see in person in more than 40 years.

Yet back in 1970 the only way in New York you could see the World Cup from Mexico was via closed circuit television in Madison Square Garden. How much we can now watch is one element of the story. More important is that on so many of those TV screens, so many American players, good American players are on view. No matter how much you watched of the 1970 World Cup (or 1974 or 1978 or 1982 or 1986 . . .), you couldn't see an American.

Now there are not only good young Americans all over Major League Soccer but on a US World Cup team so close to reaching the 2002 semifinals (on TV), a US Under 20 team which beat Argentina in the FIFA U20 world championship (on TV) and Americans playing all over the leagues of England, Germany, Holland and so on (and you can sit at home and watch them on TV).

Back then senior US squads were beaten by Bermuda, youth teams would have lost 10–0 to anyone and that is not a criticism of the youth of the day, just plain fact. As Roger Bannister, the first sub-4 minute miler once said: "I pass people every day who could have done the same, given the opportunity." Well, today's young Americans have been given the opportunity and are taking it.

I came across an old set of quotes from Sven Goran Eriksson, then England's manager, on how he viewed an upcoming game against the USA at Giants Stadium. "Playing the USA in their own country is a big test," he said. "They are an excellent team who have made enormous progress and were very unlucky not to make the semifinals of the last World Cup." This is the USA that Svennis is talking about. The US of A— that country which not so long ago was said to be a nation which could not play soccer, would not like soccer and which would be better off without soccer.

Indeed, the first time I met Svennis (who, incidentally, I strongly recommended for the US national team coaching position before the 1994 World Cup), when he was coach of Portugal's Benfica the first time around, anyone who spoke in such terms about the USA would have been looked at somewhat pitiably. But going further back than that early meeting in Lisbon, anyone who talked about the USA producing players of quality, anyone who talked of converting vast swathes of American youth, anyone who talked of holding a World Cup in the USA, anyone who even talked in their sleep of the USA winning the World Cup one day was looked upon as beyond help.

Well, some of us did talk about those things and all but one have happened in our lifetimes and maybe that missing one, the last in line, will have happened before I become too doddery to notice. Consider the poor 2006 performances as merely a dip in the road.

One of the things we did NOT talk about was women's soccer. Girls did not play soccer in the traditional soccer countries, at least not without difficulty and, at best, male condescension. When England played Scotland once upon a time, the teams were subject to considerable media ridicule although, in photographs, the England captain with the wonderful name of Nettie Honeyball looks quite proud and confident.

She must have looked down with considerable satisfaction when the seeds of soccer fell among America's athletic females who took the game as their own and raised it high enough to win the newly-introduced FIFA Women's World Cup, an Olympic Gold Medal and to raise the interest and participation in women's soccer globally.

So when, rather than if, the USA wins the World Cup one day, it will be the absolute peak of achievement in so relatively few years from the barren days when players were few in number, even lower in ability, soccer stadia were unknown, TV was empty of the game and not one soccer shirt or pants or socks or boots were manufactured or advertised in the entire country. No soccer mom had yet been born. Altogether it sometimes makes me feel like a Pony Express rider who is still around when e-mail becomes the norm.

So when that winning day comes, it will be a triumph for that chosen squad on that wonderful day but also a triumph for many unknowns who did the work and made the sacrifices (and had a lot of fun) for the sake of, the love of, their game. I hope some of the stories and some of the people are still remembered on that day; not belittled by the passionless corporate suits who speak as if there was no game before they came on the scene; and not, figuratively speaking, left begrimed and ignored on a patch of untended grass in Miami.

LAST MAN OUT,
TURN OFF THE LEAGUE

AND THEN THERE were two.

Two of just about everything, it seemed. Two floors of offices in midtown Manhattan, cavernous and almost empty of people; two executives, to give the final instructions; two secretaries, to take the final memos and then file and forget them; two lawyers, to give the last rites with legal propriety.

And two clubs; Minnesota Strikers and Toronto Blizzard, all that was left of the North American Soccer League, the league that lost its way, lost its head and in the end became the league that died of fame. It was time to go.

So anything worth keeping for posterity was shipped to the US Soccer Hall of Fame in upstate Oneonta; the furniture was sent where all forgotten office furniture goes; everyone was unemployed and 19 years of labor was over and done with. It was, in itself, a failed entity. It was, in its effect, a success.

It had wafted the spores of the universal infection called soccer across the nation; there to multiply and spawn the phenomena of soccer moms, of millions of kids, of soccer equipment everywhere and anywhere you want it, of world championships being played on its soil, of American women winning world championships and American men playing with and against the best teams and the best players the established soccer world could provide.

It used to take me about 20 minutes to drive to see my grandson play in his American Youth Soccer Organization team and along the way, if we meandered just a little, we passed 23, count them 23, soccer fields, covered with kids of all sizes, ages and both sexes playing soccer. That is not abnormal. It is rare to be able to drive anywhere in this land now without seeing the green grass of America, lined crisply for our game, with our goalposts set in American soil and looking completely at home.

I feel that a molecule of all those fields of grass belong to me and I'm sure that most people from the North American Soccer League feel the same way about all those places, dotted all over the country; places whose soil had never been touched by a soccer ball when we began in 1967. Just think on that, those thousands upon thousands of acres of American soil where that ball now bounces naturally and normally, as if at home with itself and its surroundings, yet where, until the decades beginning in the 1970s, it had not once touched or been touched.

To say that all this was planned down to the last detail by those of who built the NASL would be stretching the point. We didn't even contemplate the dramatic rise in women's soccer worldwide, with the US leading the way, but sitting on cheap flights, living in the cheapest motels and with free office space in the bowels of a baseball stadium we set down so many things as articles of faith and articles to be acted upon—so many things that came to pass. The development of the game, especially the youth game, was one of the first and considered to be an even more important task for our coaches and players than playing professional soccer. At the other extreme we said we would host a World Cup in the USA. And in between . . . well, we shall see; see what was planned and see what really happened.

The year when we decided we would eventually host a World Cup in the USA was 1969 when you could buy the US World Cup TV rights for little more than the annual contribution allowed for your IRA (which is what we did) and it would have been a laughable, hilarious thought that millions in the nation would set their alarms for the middle of the night to awaken and watch the World Cup of 2002 from Japan and Korea. Hilarious. But it happened. It is happening and it will happen, this infiltration of the world game into the nation and the affection of so many Americans for the game, to watch it to a degree, to play it in endless numbers and ever-greater ability.

None of it would have happened without the NASL. None of it. How else could it have happened, by osmosis? By millions of parents waking up one morning and saying in unison: "I think I'll start coaching soccer"? By young athletes who had never before seen a soccer ball suddenly wanting to buy one? Well, on that score, they would have been out of luck because there was only one store in the east selling soccer balls in those days.

So if the NASL had the right ideas; the right ideas and a clear view to the future, why isn't it around today? Because nothing truly prepared us for the massive leap from obscurity to success; from three paragraphs at the bottom of an inside page to headlines on the main sports page; from crowds so sparse you could almost be on a first name basis with them to crowds in the thirty thousands, forty thousands, sixties, seventy thousands from Seattle and Vancouver to Minnesota and Tampa Bay and, of course, New York. Well, actually New Jersey to be precise, Giants Stadium, where teams bearing the name of New York are sent to play because there is nowhere on the other side of the Hudson River on which to play.

Nothing truly prepared us for the onslaught of ownership which came when we expanded too fast and gathered in the egomaniacs who saw those giant crowds at Giants Stadium, couldn't afford a franchise in any established sport (and probably would not have been let in, anyway) and said "that's for me, its cheap and it must be easy if those guys can do it."

We were famous. We were cheap. We'd take anybody, well almost anybody; we turned down one man. They saw only the big crowds and the celebrities who flocked to games in so many cities. They didn't see, or want to see, the work behind it all; the consistency we had tried to maintain, the relationships within the game we had nurtured. We were a different league then, a different league every year with different attitudes and ideas and we could not survive. We were too famous for our own good and our fame was high on glamour and low on substance. Go behind the lights, wipe off the make up, take off the costumes and underneath the sickness had taken hold and was now terminal.

Thus, in the spring of 1985, when the season should have been upon us, with spring training and season ticket sales and new signings and old favorites about to perform, it was time to go, just a few weeks short of that April date back in 1967 when CBS turned on the cameras, referee Peter Rhodes blew the whistle and Baltimore played Atlanta in the first game. So, I shut the door and left, the last out after so many years and so many tales after having been, once upon a time, the first in.

THIS CHAP COX SAYS
THERE WILL BE A PRO SOCCER
LEAGUE IN AMERICA

FIRST IN AND last out and all because of Bill Cox, a man you never hear mentioned any more. Of the foreign legion, referred to later in some quarters as the British Mafia, I was indeed the first in and last out; all because, at the one end, the *Daily Express* (then, at 4.5 million a day, the largest circulation newspaper in the English-speaking world with your less-than-humble correspondent as their #1 soccer writer) sent me to North America for a few weeks and, at the other end, I was elected President of a league I could not save. But its job was done and there was drama and excitement in between, so there's nothing to be sad about.

Back in 1961 the only thing on my mind was the next story, writing about it, not being part of it. I covered the assassination of the dictator Rafael Trujillo in the Dominican Republic, although that, of course, was not on the original agenda; the Canada Cup with Sam Snead and Jimmy Demaret and Peter Alliss at Dorado Beach in Puerto Rico, an Archie Moore world title fight at the old Madison Square Garden, four sub-minute milers in an Oxford-Cambridge, Harvard–Yale track meet at Harvard—and soccer.

Up in Canada there was the Eastern Canadian Soccer League with such British luminaries on loan as Stanley Matthews, not yet a knight of the realm, and Danny Blanchflower and Malcolm Allison while down in New York, with a game in Chicopee, Mass, for heaven's sake, was the International Soccer League at the now long-demolished Polo Grounds. And Bill Cox.

William D. Cox, Yale, former timber man, philatelist of note, once owner of baseball's Philadelphia Phillies, until Major League Baseball banned him for betting on the game, ran the International Soccer League with one eye on New York's ethnic groups and the other eye on every penny.

But his mind was way ahead of such things, to the day, as he would tell me, when the USA would have its own bona fide professional soccer league. And Bill was there, front and center, when that day came. Front and center and without the finances to make it happen for him; or, for a while, so it seemed, for me; as you will see.

Over the years, Bill would drop in to see me at the black box of the *Daily Express* building in Fleet Street to tell me of the teams he was taking for the next version of the ISL, and it led to a few small stories, but then in the spring of 1966 he arrived with a whole new bunch of Americans in tow, with the story he had told me five years earlier now coming to life.

There would be a league in 1967, for sure, and, here, for a start, were Robert Hermann and Charlie Haughton from St Louis, MO to prove it, followed by Dick Cecil from Atlanta, GA and Toby Hilliard and Joe O'Neill from Midland, TX by way of Oakland, CA and more.

The trickle of the months before World Cup 1966 was as nothing compared to the flood that followed. Directed by Bill, they all came to see me and the stories flowed, though not with the same intensity and interest, of course, as the stories of the World Cup, played in our own backyard— and won, of course, by my own country—nor its aftermath when English football, indeed the whole country, glowed with pleasure.

However, as the stories flowed, so did the phone calls from coaches and players intrigued by the American effort and interested in—what else—jobs. I forget them all now but remember the first—Phil Woosnam, then a player with West Ham United, with great ambitions and an almost mystic belief in soccer in the USA. Well, he is Welsh, after all, and they're a mystic race.

We met in his car, parked in a side road off Fleet Street, the area where all the many daily newspapers of Britain were published in those days, neither of us even giving a thought to the fact that we would be side-by-side for so many years and of one mind for many of them. Phil was soon fixed up in Atlanta as general manager, coach and player, an unusual combination; but that's Phil for you; unusual for being one of the very few professionals in the UK with an University degree; unusual, for a time before he turned pro, in being regarded as the, ahem, highest paid amateur in the game (amateurs being those who play for nothing, you see). The old, brown clippings are there in front of me now

WOOSNAM LEADS BRAIN DRAIN, says the headline on a story about the first group of managers/coaches flying out to look for or land jobs. US CHASING 100 STARS, says another. But it was after the World Cup that my own casual, reporting interest in the venture changed. After the World Cup, three things coincided.

First, it was boring, deadly dull after the incredible adventure of the World Cup; I had done all I wanted to do as a journalist, at least for a while. It was, in the English idiom "After the Lord Mayor's Show" the annual and ancient parade in London of magnificent coaches and many horses, and you know what's left behind after many horses have passed by. Second, the American visits increased and Bill asked me if I would take on some actual tasks . . . and be paid for it. I accepted and so began my transition from observer to perpetrator. Third, all the other newspapers started to realize that these American-type stories Toye had been writing in the *Express* were true, really true, so we'd better wake up and start covering them, too. So, from *The Times* to the *Telegraph, Mirror* to *Mail, Herald* to *Sketch,* the stories grew, the headlines got bigger, ambition knew no bounds and success was assured. Everyone said so, everyone now took this seriously with the *Daily Mirror* firmly forecasting that the US would win the World Cup in 1982 "now that the Yanks are taking the game seriously." From zero to world champions inside 15 years? Only in the newspapers, folks, only in the newspapers.

It was not long before my wife Chris and I said to ourselves—well, if they're prepared to pay me and I'm helping send all these people to America and I'm bored stiff with the old routine, why don't we go to America. Just for two years. It will be an adventure and at worst I will come back a better journalist for the experience. So, I told Bill and he offered me the PR job with the Hartford Mules and I quit the *Express*, to everyone's absolute astonishment, and went to my farewell party on December 8, 1966, with a host of Fleet Street's sporting editors and writers present, at the Albion, in Ludgate Circus, down the hill from St Paul's Cathedral and a phone call came in for me.

It was Derek Liecty, a former employee of Bill Cox's, a friend of mine and the new general manager of one of the clubs, the Oakland Clippers. What are you going to do now, he asked? What do you mean, I said.

You haven't heard? he said. Heard what? Bill couldn't come up with the money, Hartford isn't going to be in the league.

I think I could have drunk the Albion dry that night without it having any effect but the next day dawned, as it usually does, and more offers came in—from St Louis, from New York, from the League Office, from the Oakland Clippers and from Jerry Hoffberger and the Baltimore Bays. They were all offers of PR jobs, a job I had never done before, except for the offer from Baltimore, which was for the post of General Manager, a job I had never done before even less than I had never done a PR job before. So, I took it.

It did not matter to me, nor did it to the many already packing their bags for America or hoping someone would ask, that FIFA, that august ruling body of the world game, had declared our league "outlaws" because the less-than-august US ruling body had taken money from another group to declare them (the United Soccer Association) as the rec-ognized, the only recognized, league. Phooey, we all said. What's banish-ment compared to excitement?

If the term "new world" had never been coined before, I would have thought of it now. From one side of the action, writing, to the other side, doing, and from one side of the ocean to the other and a hasty trip to New York to attend a meeting with CBS to discuss the prospect of televising league games. CBS had broadcast the England-West Germany World Cup Final, with numbers that surprised them, and now, like so many of the owners were trying to see how well that world event transmogrified (meaning to change or alter greatly and often with grotesque or humorous effect) into local action.

All was going well until Bill McPhail, then head of CBS Sports, asked: OK, how do we stop the game for commercials? You don't, I said, you can't change soccer, television will have to change. Stunned silence. Shuffling of paper. Pitying looks. That can never happen, said one of McPhail's minions. McPhail himself seemed too nice a man to want to humiliate me but I didn't feel humiliated in the least and knew, with the arrogance of youth (not that I've changed much over time), that I was right. And, of course, in the end I was; though it took a while.

After that trip, let's see now, what do we need to do next? Hmm, well the first game is less than four months away, so, what about a few players? My first scouting trip was just down the road, well the London Under-ground to be factual, to West Ham United to sign the Australian son of

Polish refugees, Karl Minor, on the recommendation of his manager Ron Greenwood, who could not get a work permit for him in the UK.

That was easy, then, so emboldened by success the next trip was a little further, off to Rio de Janeiro. To Brazil and, of course, Brazilians. I swear that there is no such thing as a single Brazilian baby. Brazilians are born in groups, talking, gesticulating, smiling, patting, circulating, coalescing and separating but always in groups. Brazilians are the most unselfconscious, least private people I have ever come across and this trip, building the 1967 Baltimore Bays, gave me my first, firm and lasting experience of their generous, gregarious nature.

We had gone, Doug Millward, the Bays coach and I, to Rio de Janeiro at the behest of Fernando Azevedo, a Brazilian front player who had been with Millward at St. Mirren, in Scotland. Fernando, having first assured himself of a Bays contract, lined up a try-out game for us across the bay in the working class suburb of Niteroi and off we went on the ferry, with all the workers homeward bound, not knowing what awaited us . . . which was, in fact, a very well-organized game with about 30 professional Brazilian players, all anxious to get to America.

We made our choices and all of us, everyone one of us, crowded into one locker room where we read off the names of the chosen—Jardel, Uriel da Veiga Fontoura, Hipolito Chilinque, Nelio dos Santos, Jose Badu da Cruz (those Brazilian names are as extravagant as their owners are gregarious)—and asked them to meet us at the hotel, the Copacabana Palace.

We set aside two rooms for our task. One would have coffee and pastries and somewhere for the players, their fathers, uncles, agents, friends to sit and wait (for we had already learned the reality of "there is no lone Brazilian") and the other room for Doug Millward and me to take each player, one by one, and try to negotiate a deal.

That plan soon came awry. We made an offer to the first one brought into the negotiating room—and as soon as we mentioned a figure, $8,000 a season or thereabouts, he (and I think the first one was Uriel) went to the connecting door and announced to the waiting masses what he had been offered . . . at which point a couple more came into our quiet room, followed by a few more, until the waiting room was empty except for a few hangers-on munching away at whatever food was left. Everybody else was in the quiet room—about 20 Brazilians all discussing every aspect of every offer and two bemused Englishmen wondering where it had all gone wrong.

Eventually, there was common agreement on how much each was worth, all within our pay scale—except for Jardel. He was, indeed, the best player, with a pedigree which included a recent stint at one of the top clubs, Flamengo. But he wanted $12,000, two thousand over our limit. He left. He came back. He left again. His compatriots looked at us imploringly. He came back. And finally he left and we had a bunch of Brazilians who helped take us to the first championship game of this new venture.

Scouting in Corsica did not have the same charm. Michel Hidalgo, later coach of France, took me there to look at an AS Monaco player in a game against Ajaccio, but it was the outside right of Ajaccio, Marc Kanyan, from the Pacific islands of New Hebrides and later of the French Olympic team, who took the eye.

After the game, we strolled down into town, sat at an outside café, sipping Ricard and smoking Gauloises among a group of club officials and fans, all of whom should have been extras in Casablanca and any other Humphrey Bogart movie of that era, and they asked—who do you like? Kanyan, I said. A widening of the eyes in shock. A few sounds more like grunts than laughs. "He is their favorite," whispered Hidalgo, "don't say that again." And with the aplomb of someone who just knows that Casablanca would have been a better movie with him in it, one of them drew his hand slowly across his throat.

Next stop Madrid and, among a handful of signings, the distinct pleasure and surprise of being able to sign Juan Santisteban, a midfielder of great skill who had won a European Cup Champions' medal with Real Madrid only two years before, and then an even greater pleasure and surprise back in London when Dennis Viollet came calling, one of the great players of the great Manchester United team, now with Stoke City in the top league but looking for new experiences and new adventure. Well, he got them and, in the meantime, we had a team; a team for a league which had not yet started life, for a club in a city I had not yet seen. Pretty dumb when you stop to think about it.

IF THE GOALPOSTS
HADN'T ARRIVED,
THIS WOULD BE A SHORT BOOK

OPENING DAY, 1967, versus Atlanta Chiefs at Memorial Stadium, Baltimore, with nationwide network TV coverage from CBS and their big name announcer Jack Whittaker on hand to give it importance, and Danny Blanchflower, late of Tottenham Hotspur and Northern Ireland, to do the color.

Opening ceremonies planned, with our multinational players to march on carrying their nation's flag, handing them over and then lining up behind our lone American, Joey Speca, behind the Stars and Stripes. Out there, too, were a bevy of Maryland beauties, in our team colors, prancing as the PA system belted out our theme song which started grandly: "It's a gold, gold and red, gold and red world when the Baltimore Bays come on."

Emotional was not the word; it was stomach-churning, tear-jerking; here we were, with this motley crew from all over, about to play a game, an actual game, and we'd done it all in a few frantic scouting trips and less than three months since we first set foot in Baltimore. My wife Chris reminds me that she was so emotional about it that she sat in the stands frozen stiff by feeling, not by cold, with her hands clenched and immoveable.

Behind it all, that day, there was another little problem. We didn't have the goalposts. They hadn't arrived and didn't until the morning of the game, from Germany, I think it was, via New York and the store of Max Doss. We hadn't forgotten, it's simply that in the US of A in those days there were no neighborhood soccer stores, no manufacturer of soccer equipment anywhere in the country, no soccer gear in the sporting good stores, no nothing. A US company, with whom the Orioles did business, tried their best but what we got was shorts baggy enough for two people and shirts of a heavy, thick material better for wearing in an NFL game in Green Bay in the winter than in the sweltering heat of an American summer.

Max Doss, on East 86th Street in New York, in the area then known as Yorkville and an aromatic amalgam of German, Hungarian, Rumanian restaurants and delicatessens, had the only soccer store on the Eastern seaboard and for a swathe of country as far west as Detroit, and that's who finally came to our rescue. The soccer loyalists in East "Bawlmer," as the locals call it, at Catonsville Community College and even the Naval Academy at Annapolis, used local carpenters' efforts, or the bottom part of American Football goalposts, with the uprights sticking way up above the soccer rectangle. Not what we wanted portrayed on national television.

I felt a fellowship with the Richard III of Shakespeare . . . a horse, a horse, my kingdom for a horse. Our salvation took so long to arrive, it might have been on Richard's horse, but it got there, otherwise I would not be telling this tale.

I had not won my argument with CBS over the insertion of commercials but I had not quite lost it, either. We would not stop the game; we would simply elongate its natural pauses. So the referee was wired for sound and given the word to pass on the word to goalkeepers to take a long time over goal kicks, for throws-in to become studies in still-life and for players knocked to the ground and hurt a little to stay down for a little rest. As a compromise it worked but it was a compromise both sides disliked intensely.

Asher Welch, one of our identical twins from Jamaica (well, one of them had a small spot somewhere on his face, I think it was Asher), crossed the ball from the left, Guy "Smiler" St Vil from Haiti darted into the box and headed it in and there it was, victory over Atlanta Chiefs in front of 8434 spectators, a national TV audience and The Great Adventure was under way. But I get ahead of myself. The culture shock for all of us descending on America must have been severe. It certainly was from our side of the divide.

From a world where football meant only one thing, where the word soccer was synonymous with it and there was not a soul who was not aware of the game, to a place where it was so hidden in tiny enclaves that the Maryland National Bank listed my employer as Baltimore Boys' Supper Club instead of Baltimore Bays Soccer Club. Then there was the matter of distances. We knew America was big, but this big? I had a call from some soccer enthusiasts somewhere in North Carolina, would we send a team down to play an exhibition game, they were so excited about it.

So, I looked at the map, saw that North Carolina was only a couple of States away and sent Dennis Viollet in charge of three cars of players for the little jaunt down south. Dennis was a nice man but not so nice when he returned to tell me they had driven like maniacs, changed in the cars and got to the field as the other team was about to quit and go home. Yes, America is a big country.

More serious were the vestiges of segregation. We had players of all hues and we had the works of the world to find an apartment complex that would take white and black and brown in the same building. Try sorting out those color striations with a bunch of Brazilians. Mind you, our own welcome was hardly with bands and flowers at the airport to greet us. Arriving in a strange city in a strange land to do a strange job, Christine, 7-year-old Gaynor and 1-year-old Robert, and I were delivered to a very utilitarian motel in Timonium, Maryland; I was given, loaned, a car, automatic (which was new to me) and which, of course, insisted on being driven on the wrong side of the road, and told the way to Memorial Stadium. Some of the furniture at the motel was held together by tape and no one had even thought to provide milk or juice or bread or baby food; nothing, just dumped there. And that after an 11-hour journey with two kids. I made sure from then on that no one, no matter from where or how humble, would ever be welcomed with lack of warmth. Lincoln Phillips, Sgt. Phillips of the Trinidad Regiment until I brought him north to play outstandingly in goal and later become a noted coach, of Howard University among others, still looks at me sideways when he tells me how his wife still remembers the flowers that greeted her on arrival. Honestly, Lincoln, it was only a courtesy, nothing more, so relax.

The next day was my "unveiling," my press conference and I have rarely felt so nervous; nervous about finding my way there, because the car still insisted on being on the wrong side of the road; nervous about meeting those who would, a few days before, have been my comrades-in-arms, the media, and nervous about making a speech; never having done so before. When the time came, I think I was almost too tired to care; leaving home, a long flight via Philadelphia with a 7-year-old and a 1-year-old, all too strange, exhausting and, in the end maybe, relaxing because I could not have written better reviews myself. I have absolutely no idea what I said, neither before, during, after nor now but it obviously went down well.

N. P. Clark, in the *News American* wrote: "He sold 'em soccer, he sold 'em the Bays, he sold 'em the Orioles, he sold 'em Toye and darned if he didn't sell 'em their own town. From a foreigner who landed less than 24 hours before it was a promotional tour de force beyond belief." The others were just as complimentary, though the honeymoon did not last the full two years of my contract with the Bays, partly because the media is, after all, the media and does not live on nice words alone; partly because of me, who, I hate to admit it, is not always sweetness and light either, usually saying what I feel and feeling what I say, and partly, maybe chiefly, because of the internal jealousies and wish that we'd be gone, emanating from many of the baseball people. I have to say, though, that overall, and I mean over all the country, that hostility towards soccer existed in the media and disappeared even more slowly than segregation and has not gone today, not at all.

None of us, I think, realized that we were coming into anything other than a friendly, welcoming environment. There was nothing wrong with the people, they were as nice or not nice as people everywhere always are; no, it was the personnel, the personnel of major league baseball and pro football, and their corps of media in the mainstream, who greeted soccer with disdain bordering on hostility.

My first club, the Bays, was owned by the Baltimore Orioles (in turn owned by National Beer, owned by Jerry Hoffberger) and we were not the only club so owned. It didn't take too long, going into Memorial Stadium every day and turning left while the Orioles people went in and turned right, to feel that this was an experiment the baseball people, with very few exceptions, devoutly wished to end as soon as possible. This was evident in many small ways but maybe this will help make it plainer. We did well in "Bawlmer" that first year, ending up in the championship series, with one of the cheapest teams in the league and with 16,000-plus for our home championship game against the Oakland Clippers.

Pretty good going, when we had started six month before as "who the hell are these guys and what is it they play?" We had actually won the divisional title in mid-air, en route from a 0–0 draw at Atlanta when the pilot radioed down to get the score of New York Generals, the only team with a chance of catching us, on the road at Oakland, found they had lost and announced it over the PA, to the politely applauding, but somewhat uncomprehending, passengers. On arrival at the gate, there was this group of fans, led by Mayor Theodore McKeldin, holding a congratulatory banner. So, we had arrived in more senses than one.

Added to that was my selection, in *The Sporting News* poll of league votes, as Executive of the Year. I was away when *The Sporting News* made the announcement and had been back several days when Bill Corcoran, the PR man who really wanted a job with the Orioles, not us, came in, put an object in brown paper on my desk and said "congratulations." For what?, I asked . . . and he told me and I unwrapped the brown paper and there was this engraved plaque from *The Sporting News.*

Nobody else bothered to mention it; not Hoffberger, not his next in line, Frank Cashen, GM of the Orioles, not Joe Hamper, Controller for both clubs and Cashen's next in line (and the man who was our welcoming committee back in January). No announcement to gain credit and news for the club, no ceremony, no nothing. Were we taking too much attention away from the Orioles? Were we getting too big for our boots? Intruding too much into the city that belonged to the Orioles and the Colts and no one else?

In any event, the year did not end well for another reason; the firing of coach Doug Millward, once a player for Alf Ramsey at Ipswich Town (in the days before money ruled all and a small club could climb through the ranks and even win the league on ability and in the days before plain Alf became Sir Alf for leading England to victory in the 1966 World Cup) and later manager of St. Mirren in Scotland. He had to go, though it isn't worth recalling all the reasons why; sufficient to say it was his comportment rather than his coaching which made him dispensable.

Our practice field was often the Norwegian Seaman's Mission field, surrounded by houses with people in them; people hearing Doug's ripe and repeated oaths at a high level of decibels through the session. That caused complaints, many of them, despite warnings. And when Joey Speca, our lone American remember, scored an absolutely glorious goal, a thunderbolt in a 3–2 win over the Philadelphia Spartans, Doug's comment to the media was along the lines of: He'll never do that again.

That did not go down too well, nor did his inevitable firing. The deed had to be done and should have been done earlier when he was offered the chance to resign with dignity and refused. But by the time it did happen, it was all the worse because Doug's son was ill in hospital by then. Nothing life-threatening but, all the same, the poor soul was ill in hospital and there must be better times at which to be fired.

We tried to keep it under our hats during that time, to relieve an additional public burden, but Doug had not been so reticent and, naturally told the story to all and sundry with his own interpretation and criticisms attached. It was Labor Day, 1967, when the news leaked out to the media. Joe Hamper called me in from a day off on the Eastern Shore somewhere and we had a lot of work to do to put forth our side of the story; what today rejoices in the name of "spin." I know the date for sure because it was my first year in the USA and I told Joe "now I know why you call in Labor Day, this is the hardest work we have done all year."

No one likes to be fired, of course, but Doug had made a meal of the situation and the timing and we were blasted up one side of Fort McHenry, where the legendary banner still waved, and down the other. It was not a good time for anyone but as a writer-turned-successful-executive, I had now learned one thing for sure. Once you know you have to do something, do it now, immediately, get it over with, the fall out may be bad but it will be a lot worse if you let it linger. Sadly, as we shall see, I forgot my own lesson at the end of my first season at Toronto Blizzard, a dozen years or so later.

Of course, those in baseball who did wish it to end in very short order soon got their wish, those who, it was plain in hindsight, had bought into pro soccer "just in case" . . . just in case it worked and became a competitor for the national pastime. In the meantime, it was a case of "the Stadium is rented, the infrastructure of marketing and promotion and PR is in place, so we won't lose much by bringing in some cheap labor from overseas, will we?"

Baltimore itself, I must say, was a dump; an interesting, unique old city allowed to become a dump though, thankfully, revived somewhat in more recent years. There were steel shutters on all the downtown stores before dusk, there were riots, only a couple of restaurants downtown were still open at night, the culinary heights rose no further than crab cakes and once, on a wedding anniversary splurge, I ordered an expensive Bordeaux red in a restaurant which boasted the Best Wine Cellar in the east (as opposed to the one which called itself the World Famous Eager House) and had it served, still unopened, in a bucket of ice. You do not, you see, drink expensive red wine frozen cold; it must be opened to the air, to breath to luxuriate the senses—not dumped in a pale of ice like a six pack of Bud.

At one formal, tuxedo and black tie banquet I attended, all the people around me carried bottles of booze in brown paper bags in their pockets and poured the only alcohol available into the water glasses. When the food arrived, the waitresses stood at the end of the long tables and had the guests pass the plates . . . and pass the dirty plates back to her later. From London with its culture and sophistication to a city whose downtown closed before dusk, whose glorious waterfront was ruined by neglect, whose race relations were abominable, was a chastening move. One police officer invited me out in his patrol car one night when he was due to be in black west Baltimore so I could see the excitement. "You should see the way your shoes shine when you kick their heads and the blood spills out," is the way he put it. It's the truth.

This was all the more difficult to comprehend when you consider that back in London, the huge lights over one theatre in the West End advertised Agatha Christie's play *The Ten Little Niggers* and in every shoe shop one of the shades of footwear available was labeled Nigger Brown. The "n" word carried no venom; it was just one of the many derogatory terms people used about each other in those far off days before political correctness was known. We called everyone mildly derogatory names—Jock, Paddy, Taffy for the Scots, Irish and Welsh; the English were, according to Australians, Pommy Bastards and the prevailing jokes ended by insulting the listener and his origins. (Not long after writing this, I came across a story in an English newspaper, reporting that a man had been fined about $400 for calling a Welshman Taffy; what was normal once, now a crime.)

Tom Shelford, Lance Corporal, Royal New Zealand Signals, my Maori friend with whom I shared many an electrifying dispatch run over the frozen hills and streams of Korea and teacher of the vilest Maori insults, said he and his mates had always thought of Britain as one place and they were all astonished at how regional we were, in accent and in often dismissive names for people from a different part of the same country. I know that sometimes when people in my part of the country spoke about foreigners (bleddy vurriners, is how it came out) they were likely to be talking about people from London, or the Midlands or, even worse, the North of England. So, political correctness was a term no one had come upon yet, though Agatha Christie's play is now probably called *Ten Height-Disadvantaged Dark Skinned Indigenous People.*

There were, in addition, Wogs, Yids, Wops and Dagos, all somewhat more derogatory, but the only truly insulting epithets were reserved for the French, Frogs, and Germans, Krauts; for nationalities, not color. The feelings aroused by the "n" word were a total shock.

There were of course, more laughable differences in the meaning of words and phrases, which our new coach in 1968, Gordon Jago, brought out from the London club, Fulham, later owned by the owner of Harrods, Mohamed al Fayed, father of Dodi, Princess Diana's companion on the night of their fatal crash, found out when finishing a rousing speech to a large audience with the cry: Up The Bays. As I suspect explanation is needed . . . in England, this is a rallying cry of support and fidelity to the team in question . . . in the USA, it is rude, an insult and, depending on the circumstances, the prelude to a punch-up, a brawl, a fracas; use the one you like.

All part and parcel of early misunderstandings and smiles with confusion over things like: Shall I knock you up in the morning? (meaning a wake up call on the door or getting you pregnant, depending on where it is said) or the use of the word "bomb." Say that in England and means a big success; say that in the USA and it means a failure. I suspect that may be because on one side of the water, we saw a lot of bombs and when they landed lots bricks and mortar and bodies around them, went UP. On the other side of the water, most people have only seen bombs on TV and in the movies when they were on the way DOWN.

So many daily words gave instant recognition to the phrase of Winston Churchill's—two nations separated by a common tongue. On day 2 in America, my wife desperately needed to get something in which to deposit our hefty 1-year-old son Robert (later to do much walking on his own in the 3rd Battalion, 8th Regiment, USMC), rather than carry him everywhere. So she got a cab into Towson and went into the biggest department store and asked where were the prams. She might as well have asked for the cure to the common cold but eventually she explained that this was something in which you pushed kids around. Ah, a stroller! Of course, but in the UK pram is short for perambulator (which is highfalutin' language for walking about) and is exactly that, a stroller.

Told that strollers were upstairs, my wife asked where were the lifts? Well, once that had been translated into elevators, she bought a pram and came back down in the lift and over time we became able to switch back and forward in two versions of the language. Though I still don't think it look right to spell words like color, neighbor, harbor without a "u" after the "o." If it wasn't for this damned computer and its green lines underneath words it doesn't like, there would be "u's" all over the place.

As if English-English and American-English translations were not bad enough, we had many players who spoke no English at all and no English-speaking players who spoke a word of Spanish or Portuguese or French. Enter Mr Costa, a kindly old Brazilian gentleman, resident in

Maryland and willing, nay anxious, to help out. It was amusing to see half a squad of grown men intently listening, shouting and doing so in a semblance of a soccer game, shouting "my ball" or "behind you" or "far post." Somehow, the phrase "behind you" struck a chord with so many of the non-English-speaking players that it became a catch-phrase of its own . . . "behind you" came to serve as "good morning" or "how are you" or "what about a cup of coffee." Anyone listening in would have thought they had gone mad. But anyone listening to Mr Costa's serious translation efforts could only have become worried because it went as follows:

A player with a contract or personal issue would speak, in whatever was his native tongue, and Mr Costa would turn to me and speak—not in English but in same language the player had spoken. Harmless and good for a laugh, yes, until you looked at the player's face and saw his concern as he began speaking firmly to Mr Costa again and you eventually realized that not only had Mr Costa not spoken to you in the right language (English for me), he had not even spoken the right message in the language he had been supposed to translate.

While we had ample evidence of racial problems in the USA, we had plenty of skin shades in our teams, though not yet any black Americans, that was yet to come. It made me wonder then, as now, what it was that made the biggest clubs in Europe ignore black players, for the most part, for so long. Benfica's great team of the 1960s was replete with African players, as was the Portuguese national team because in those days Angola and Mozambique were still Portuguese colonies and their magnificent players, Eusebio and Mario Coluna among them, were qualified to play only for Portugal.

But black players hardly ever made it north of the Pyrenees. Was it color or was it where they came from that caused this barrier? By that, I give a quote as illustration, from Joe Richards, from Barnsley, a less than idyllic town in industrial Yorkshire and never one of the great clubs. At the time he was President of the Football League in England and Chairman of the England Selection Committee, a crusty old self-made man with a Yorkshire accent and archaic phrasing on occasion.

We were on the plane home from the World Cup in Chile in 1962 and Joe Richards said to me: Yon Peel (yes Peel, not Pele) would never make it in England, with all our different conditions. He'd never be any good in the muck in the winter in Barnsley. Not that he was black, mind you, but he couldn't do his stuff away from what was simply thought of as perfect fields and perfect weather wherever Peel and the like came from. Was color a factor? I have no idea.

Early on, Phil Woosnam, who had been on coaching clinics in Africa, signed Willie Evans, as tough a center half as you could find, from Ghana, and a 17-year-old from Jamaica, Allan "Skill" Cole, who could have risen to the heights if he hadn't gone home, grown luxuriant dreadlocks and become one of Bob Marley's crowd. Phil persuaded one of his old clubs, Aston Villa, to give two others a try when there was no more work for them in Atlanta—Freddie Mwila, a truly skilled attacking midfielder from Zambia, and later their national coach for a spell, and Emment Kapengwe also from Zambia, as aggressive a front player as you could find.

Today, a color and climate of origin no longer matter, black players— imported, immigrant sons and now native-born, proliferate and succeed handsomely. Today Freddie and Emment would have stayed there at Villa Park. Then, they passed on home after a few weeks. Mind you, in the US of A, one early owner, who stayed with us only a while, looked at my multicolored Bays team, leaned over and said: "Well, they have skill, but you can't trust the jigs when it gets tough."

Rotten stuff and disproved in war and sport. I hope this doesn't make me sound like a raging liberal. I am not. My politics range somewhere in between Conservative and Anarchist but the truth's the truth. My Anarchist tendencies always arise when I am listening to a politician.

We were dragged to a meeting with a prominent politician when time came for a return trip to Atlanta and a request for a photo op, with outside right Art Welch, the other Jamaican twin, and this local big wig; an amiable half-wit, I found him to be, named Lester Maddox. I had to be told that he was the segregationist Governor of Georgia. So, in retrospect, half-wit was a compliment.

Worse, though, and more serious was our first flight for a road trip in our existence, United Airlines to Chicago to play the Chicago Spurs and crisis on landing. Shoes off, sharp objects removed, bend forward in the approved manner for an emergency landing. Zemaria, our Brazilian central defender, he of slowing legs but supreme timing, was in the bar, Scotch already sunk before the last passengers were off.

Later in the season, we played the Spurs at home and scored what was probably the fastest goal ever in world soccer. I say probably because apart from the goalscorer, Ruben Garcete, no one really saw it coming, not even the Chicago goalkeeper Manuel Camacho. He, poor soul, was somewhere mid-way between the corner flag and the goal, having a friendly chat with some spectators, when the referee blew the whistle to start the second half. Ruben Garcete, seeing an empty goal facing him 50 yards or so away, blasted it down field and into the net, as poor Camacho, alerted by sounds of alarm from his team mates, raced frantically towards the goal; too late by yards. The guess was it took four seconds and I guess you could try it yourselves and see how long it takes for a well-hit ball to travel that distance.

My media background wasn't allowed to fade into the past because I was doing the color on many Bays' telecasts on WJZ and my impertinence in suggesting CBS could not stop the game for commercials was forgotten when Danny Blanchflower had gone, to no great dismay from CBS and the League brass because he was rather more down to earth in his comments than they would have liked. So I was roped in to replace him and the atmosphere on CBS telecasts changed from the professional assessment to the promotional, sometimes too promotional, and this exchange took place:

> Play by play man, Mario Machado (substitute for Jack Whittaker): "And now, coming on the field for Kansas City is Walter McC****, one of Scotland's great players, isn't he Clive?"
> Color man Clive Toye (substitute for Blanchflower): "Well, he did play a couple of games for Motherwell." (Which is like playing a handful of games in Triple A as distinct from being MVP of the World Series.)

Blanchflower, captain of Spurs and Northern Ireland, raconteur, writer, broadcaster left his most indelible mark on the English language when he was, briefly, manager of Northern Ireland and in a team talk said: "They'll try to kick you all over the park today so make sure you get your retaliation in first."

I was pressed into service, too, to write the first book in the USA on soccer for kids, to explain the world game to them. But first explain it to the editor at Franklin Watts, publisher of that first book. "You have to make changes, you're making lots of errors—for instance, you say this team is one of the big ones in Argentina so you can't call River Plate by an English name, its Rio de la Plata," she said. Took a lot of convincing, much harder than writing it, that so many clubs have English names because they were started by British sailors, merchants, teachers, settlers (River Plate, Newells Old Boys, Everton, Arsenal, Wanderers, Liverpool, Corinthians are just some of the names existing today in Argentina, Brazil and Uruguay for example). All that work for $500.

ONE NATION UNDER FIFA,
ALL'S WELL IN THE WORLD . . .
FOR A WHILE

OF COURSE, IT had been a very American exuberance that had brought about, the year before, not only one professional soccer league where none had existed before but two professional soccer leagues where none existed before.

With the very successful telecast by CBS of the 1966 World Cup Final between England and West Germany added to the ages of work by Bill Cox, all manner of sports entrepreneurs had become interested and, in the manner of sports entrepreneurs, they could not agree with each other and thus here were some of the best known and wealthiest sports-minded people in America battling each other to see who would win the supposed enthusiasm and fealty of the great American public.

This was a great American sporting public, moreover, thoroughly indoctrinated and enamored by its own games of childhood with countless images of play and familiar names and moments ingrained and ingested with their mother's milk. Were they suddenly, instantaneously, going to be transformed by something new and "foreign," in this case the original football, the first to be organized with common and accepted rules, rules first written in 1863 at a meeting at a pub in London's Covent Gardens, the Freemason's Arms? Well, no, they weren't, as we know. (And, no, I wasn't there at the Freemason's Arms. My stagecoach was late.) But that didn't halt the battles between those who, for a short time, knew better.

They battled to see who could be the first to start. They battled to get recognition from the governing body of US soccer, and thus of FIFA, the world body, giving official access to players and teams and referees every-where and anywhere. They battled to get a television contract. At the time, and at a distance, I thought why on earth don't these people agree on a common course of action and build this thing together? But, then, of course, I hadn't met most of them!

Bill Cox's group, aided and abetted by yours truly, raced around signing coaches and players and showed they could begin, with their own teams and their actual own players, so the other group, the United Soccer Association, rushed to sign up entire foreign clubs to masquerade under local names so they would not be left at the post; thus, for a summer, Wolverhampton Wan-derers became Los Angeles Wolves, Stoke City became Cleveland Stokers, Shamrock Rovers became Boston Rovers and so on.

Cox's group won a TV contract, with CBS. The others had the law on their side. I did not know then, and do not know now, why the governing body, then called the United States Soccer Football Association, took the application and the money from the other group and gave them the bless-ings of officialdom. Perhaps it had something to do with the aforemen-tioned William D. Cox and the running battles he had had over the years of running the International Soccer League. Whatever the reasons, they gave the United Soccer Association (USA) league the sole right to be rec-ognized; we, the National Professional Soccer League, were the outlaws, frowned upon from on high by FIFA and banned from the game. It was a ban which had the salutary effect of a wet lettuce thrown from fifty paces, i.e. none. Coaches coached, players played, referees refereed and by the time they had done that for a season or less, reality was settling in.

The sheer idiocy of two leagues fighting for a place in the American hearts and minds came more to the pockets than the minds of those in command. It was not only that losses were now a reality but looming overhead was the reality that America's favorite pastime, litigation, was now to be brought into play. The NPSL threatened to sue, not just the United States Soccer Football Association, but also FIFA. FIFA blinked and Sir Stanley Rous, President of FIFA, whose ghost writer I had once been, called his friend, the past and future President of the USSFA, Jimmy McGuire, to get it sorted out and it was and we were one league in time for the 1968 season.

There had to be some jostling and pushing and ownership accommo-dations, especially in cities where both leagues had had clubs in 1967, and some instances of the laws of unintended consequences, for example:

Out of the blue I received a phone call from Vancouver after the Canadians merged with the San Francisco Gales, to leave room for the Oakland Clippers (and here, before your eyes glaze over at the start of this tale of merger and migration of clubs, let me say all of names and changes and appearances and disappearances and reappearances are charted in Appendix "A" at the end of the book, so relax). Said the caller: "There's two of us here, now, two coaches. They want me to stay on and the two of us work together, both of us in charge, what do you think?" No chance of that working, I said, go home.

So Ferenc Puskas, Hungarian Army officer, the Galloping Major of the Magical Magyars of the 1950s, the Hungarian superstar who had escaped during the Hungarian revolution of 1956 to become a major figure, if you'll excuse the pun, with fabled Real Madrid, stayed on to be the coach, be out of work within the year and travel, not too successfully, to put it kindly, through a succession of lesser coaching jobs in lesser lands. And home went this Geordie (there we go again, labeling someone from the north east of England with a regional name) to become manager of many, including Barcelona, PSV Eindhoven, Newcastle United and England and end his days knighted by the Queen. Sir Bobby Robson.

But, back in the land of our opportunity, we were now one league, all legal and aboveboard, all with the same objective, settling in for the long haul to build our league, build our game, build our future and the future of millions of kids who would play our game. There could not be any doubt about that, could there? After all, not only had we all gone through contortions to be a legal one league, but I was appointed Chairman of the Development Coordinating Committee, charged with coming up with the plan to settle in for the long haul, to build our league and so on and so forth and to present it to the annual meeting of 1968 at an hotel just outside Chicago's O'Hare Airport. Silly me. I did as I was asked and produced nine pages, single-spaced, though the crux of it was contained in the opening paragraphs:

"The basis of all recommendations, proposals and arguments made by this Committee is that the NASL can not afford to concern itself only with the professional affairs of the member clubs. The game of soccer has to be developed and sold at every level of life in North America so that a favorable climate is established in which we can get down to the ultimate objective of selling tickets for NASL games."

It also hit on these topics, many of which have become more familiar, indeed fact, as time has passed: . . . the general arousing of the youth leaders and youth of this country to the overall benefits of playing soccer . . . the formation of national little league championships . . . a nationwide structure of clinics for coaches . . . the national team must not be allowed to be idle in non-World Cup years. It must play against national teams on a regular basis . . . a good and improving national team is of vital importance in attracting national and international attention to the game in this country . . . a National Soccer Center is essential for the future . . . (it opened 25 years later, June 7, 2003!) . . . the champion team will take part in the CONCACAF championship . . .

It went on for nine more pages, saying how it should be done, including the need to get the game firmly into the educational system, so it gathered "snob appeal and an acceptance outside the ethnic communities." But the first two paragraphs told the tale, a tale that at the time nobody even read, as far as I know. I don't know for sure because I wasn't in the room for most of the meeting, crucial though my report was supposed to be.

By then, I had left the Bays because I did not want to extend my contract past the original two years and neither did they, so it was a perfect meeting of the minds. Bays' owner Jerry Hoffberger asked me to leave the room until it came time to discuss my report, so I did and spent the time playing putt-putt golf with Brian Glanville, football writer for so many years for one or more of the serious, heavyweight newspapers of the UK media.

Logic says that must have been a more enjoyable way to waste a day because inside the room our fearless leaders, whom I, in my innocence, thought were planning the future, a long-term future to build, were actually planning a future of a few hours. It wasn't working quickly, went the theme, so it isn't going to work at all and those same men who had so recently been fighting to be in the league, THE league, were now scrambling over each other to get to the exit first. In any event, my two years with the Bays were up. The league was in disarray, near death, maybe already breathing its last and so the hard decision for us was at hand—sell the furniture, head back to England, Home and Fleet Street or put everything in store, park ourselves with my wife Chris's sister Pearl in Boston for a while and see what happens next?

One of the things that happened next—and I don't know precisely where it was and don't know exactly when it was—but the crucial meeting was certainly the following year, when you could fit the entire Board of Directors into a modest family saloon, and attended by Phil Woosnam, Lamar Hunt, Dick Cecil, Bob Hermann and myself and we certainly made the most crucial decision.

(As an aside, Paul Tagliabue, wise and esteemed former Commissioner of the National Football League, surrounded by the wealth of ages, owners as far as the eye can see and enough staff to populate a small city, tells the tale of his first professional sports league meeting when he was but a young, aspiring lawyer: It was an NASL meeting in Atlanta in August 1969. The whole league office staff and owners met sitting around one bed in the Atlanta Marriott . . . Lamar Hunt's bed.)

However, that fateful decision was simply that the NASL's job was to make soccer grow in the country, not just make the NASL grow. The NASL, especially in view of the poor, understaffed and passive Federation, was to be the nucleus of all activity and so it was. The nine pages of the mostly unread report of 1968 was now NASL gospel. Preparing for and playing in professional soccer games thus became an adjunct to the development work, the missionary work—and kids are playing today because of the groundwork laid by journeymen pros from overseas whose names they never knew.

Some went home when their time was up, many stayed on and still are dotted around the country, running youth leagues, holding camps, still working for the future when the future they helped to build is already here. Some stayed on and became prominent and successful as coaches—coaches who spent more time propagating the game than they did coaching their own teams.

Gordon Bradley comes to mind. He started with one Cosmos Coaches Corner in 1971—one group, one night a month. By the time he was through, there were more than 40 Coaches Corner all over the tri-state area and not even Gordon could get to all those meetings, so out night after night trotted the players. Gordon did more clinics and speeches and exhortation on behalf of the game in half-a-year than all those who followed him did in entirety. Ron Newman is another. They'll be closing the lid on Ron and he'll be talking soccer to the pall bearers and trying to get a quick game of 3-a-side. Tales are told of Ron, player at Atlanta, coach of Dallas and San Diego, Miami and Kansas City, of seeing a bunch of kids kicking a ball as he was driving by, stopping and getting out to give them an impromptu clinic, pushing some parents into organizing a team and joining a league. If the grass and the trees aren't playing soccer, its not Ron's fault; they must have heard him often enough.

The sorrow which followed Clive Charles' death from cancer in 2004 is testament to the players in Portland who grew, in personal and football terms, from the dedication of this one-time West Ham United full back. But this was 1968, remember, when that plan was first put forward. Who knows how much further the game may have progressed if those measures had been implemented then. Instead, the agenda was focused on survival, not the future, and the future was pretty dim.

ANYONE ALIVE IN THERE?

IT WAS NOT luxurious but it certainly was large, the League office which Phil Woosnam and I opened in the early months of 1969. Free, too, because by the courtesy of the Atlanta Chiefs, who were owned by the Atlanta Braves, by far the most supportive of the baseball/soccer owners, we were parked in one corner of the baseball visitors' locker room at Atlanta Stadium. Where the stars of the National League had trodden, sweated, cursed and celebrated, we sat and thought.

We had more than enough furniture, masses of it from the League office last seen in more traditional corporate quarters in Manhattan which in itself, of course, had been the merger of the offices of two competing leagues. We had telephones and typewriters. We had Phil as Executive Director, myself as Director of Administration and Information; we had another Briton, Eddie Pearson, as part-time Referee-in-Chief and eventually we had Jana Falzarano as secretary. Three-and-a-half people and five clubs, all the rest departing after that owners meeting in Chicago when I presented the development plan that nobody read.

And we had all the ideas in the world. That is where we talked of the future; there and on a park bench downtown where we would grab a sandwich for lunch. There we planned the future league; expanded of course, with a jewel of a club in New York, Pele to play for it, a World Cup held in the USA, millions of American kids playing the game and many of them playing it well, really well, in the League and for the USA in the World Cup.

We were planning for the Federation, too; a Federation then in one office in the Empire State Building and so short of cash and assets that when one of the youth teams was playing in a FIFA tournament in Canada and had to change uniforms because of a clash of colors, they had to borrow a spare set from, of all people, the Cuban team. The national body's only employee was the General Secretary, Joe Barriskill, a peppery old soul, who ran the game in the USA in his spare time from being a steward in the press box at Yankee Stadium, you know, baseball. (Can anyone of the very many employed now at Soccer House, the governing body's elegant, grand, indeed magnificent, edifice, in Chicago, even imagine it?)

When we sometimes shared our plans, hopes, beliefs, we were met with, shall we say a reluctance to take us seriously; none more so than when we convinced the Federation to declare it a matter of policy that the aim was to host the World Cup of 1978, then nine years hence. We even issued a press release about it, which I wrote in my capacity as Chairman of the USSF Promotion and Publicity Committee (meaning my labor was free as there was no money to hire anyone), but I don't think anyone ever used it or read it, except us and except now because here it is in all its historic glory:

SOCCER: AMBITION UNLIMITED
AND A MAJOR PROGRAM NOW UNDER WAY

NEW YORK, NEW YORK

The most ambitious development program in an American sport has, as its ultimate target, the hosting of the world's largest single-sport tournament . . . the World Cup of Soccer.

The United States Soccer Football Association's newly-formed National Development Committee has recommended to its National Commission that a bid be made for the 1978 World Cup finals.

This bid to follow the World Cup finals of 1970 (Mexico) and 1974 (West Germany) is just one move in a dramatic National Development Plan aimed at taking soccer to every corner of the country and to every prospective player and spectator.

USSFA president Erwin Single comments: "There is every indication that for the first time soccer is being discovered from within and is no longer considered an imported sport. Participation at schools, camps and youth recreational facilities throughout the United States is now at a record high. The development plan is in the most capable hands at all levels and no effort will be spared to ensure the plan's success."

The National Development Plan, worked out at Chicago under the chairmanship of Gene Edwards of Milwaukee, calls for a 7-point approach to soccer's growth with the structure laid down prior to the appointment of a National Coach sometime within the next twelve months.

The points are:

1. To establish a national youth program—the Youth of America Soccer Program—for boys 7 to 15.
2. To increase participation at all other levels.
3. To elevate standards of playing, coaching and refereeing.
4. The development of, and competition for, United States' national teams at professional, amateur and youth levels.
5. To assist the North American Soccer League in strongly establishing a coast to coast professional league.
6. To stage an international youth tournament in the United States in 1973.
7. To apply to host the 1978 World Cup finals.

Under Chairman Edwards, First Vice President of USSFA, are five Directors . . . Harry Saunders of New York (East), George Fishwick of Chicago (Mid West), Don Greer of San Francisco (Far West), Dane Petersen of Denver (Rockies) and Clyde Partin of Atlanta (South). Phil Woosnam of the NASL and John McKeon of East Stroudsburg State college, representing college soccer, complete the National Development Committee.

So, getting the World Cup took sixteen years longer than our target year of 1978, but it happened in that glorious summer extravaganza of 1994. This was at a time when the concept of a national team was foreign to most Americans. You mean it's like an all-star team? Well, yes, but they have to be citizens of this country. Oh and the other team are citizens of the USA, too? No, they are of another country. Oh, why do we play against them, then?

I am not sure that Bruce Arena, the US national team coach for so long, and his players like Kasey Keller, Landon Donovan and Eddie Pope who, 30 years or so later were big names, earning good money, and drawing crowds of 30,000, 40,000 and 50,000 on a regular basis to watch them in the national team could comprehend such a time, either. Personally, I am not sure even now why we did it, why we stayed, why we bothered. In Phil's case there was more than a touch of that Welsh mysticism I mentioned before; he felt he had a true mission in life.

In my case, I think it was more a case of being bloody-minded; an English expression that pretty well defies translation. The nearest I can get, I think, is to say it means being stubborn to the point of stupidity. So, the mystic and the stupid decided to give it a go.

When Phil and I finally had enough loot to open an actual League office on Peachtree Street, and were, in any case, in danger of being over-whelmed as the baseball season was looming and our office was required as a locker room again, we decided to hold a press conference. It was to announce our new season, a two-part season with clubs from overseas coming in to represent our five cities in the first part of the year, followed by a normal season of our own clubs, with our own players.

So, we sent out the notices and went out to the local deli and carried in sandwiches and pastries and coffee and Coke, to save the delivery charge, and were a little concerned that we had no booze, because we could not afford it. We set it all out carefully on a large table, in my office because we only had two offices and a reception area, and waited for the multitude. Some time after the appointed hour, our concerns changed. Was no one coming, no one at all? We mused on that for awhile and then a greater concern appeared—suppose someone now came and realized that while he, or they, was, or were, late, nobody else had been?

So, Phil and I set about the table, slopping coffee and Coke into cups and glasses, tearing sandwiches and doughnuts apart and leaving the kind of debris a departed press corps might have left. We were surveying the damage when we did get a late visitor, just one, and it didn't matter. He had obviously been to places where booze was on the budget and after seeing the place empty of the further refreshment he sought, he grabbed a sandwich, a press release and left.

We now embarked upon the season and the days we almost died. This was the first day we almost died. We had brought five foreign teams over to play as home teams in each of our five cities and the first part of our two-part season was now over. It had not been rapturously received, to say the least, and we went into a League meeting with Phil and I and the five club bosses present—Lamar Hunt of Dallas, Bob Hermann of St. Louis, Dick Cecil of Atlanta, John Latshaw of Kansas City and Jerry Hoffberger of Baltimore.

The death knell was ready to be rung when Hoffberger said—we are out. We will complete this season if we have to because we said we would but I suggest we all agree right now to withdraw our performance bonds and stop right now. It needed only one more voice, one more vote and we were through, absolutely through. None came. So Jerry and my ex-club would be gone at the end of the season and we knew that four would not be enough. The hunt for more was seriously on.

When John Latshaw finally did give up his Kansas City franchise in 1971, by the way, he left behind one indelible remark. He suggested we could keep down staff and player costs by hiring their wives as domestic servants. I wonder what David Beckham's missus would think of that.

This was the second day we almost died, at a rather run-down, ratty motel under the shadows of the O'Hare Expressway in Chicago. The way we had gone about the hunt for new clubs was for me to do the initial rounds and find out if someone was really interested or not. I know I almost found a live one in Toronto in Steve Stavro, a great soccer fan, sponsor of so many teams and the man who kept Varsity Stadium alive and available for soccer for many years and later owner of the Toronto Maple Leafs of the National Hockey League.

Then I found two who were not only alive but kicking; two teams in the semipro American Soccer League, the Washington Darts and the Rochester Lancers, in a league to which Bill Cox was now paying attention. After my initial visits, I set out again, cheapest flights, no matter the hour, with Lamar Hunt for company, sharing rooms (and he still owes me for a shared razor blade at the Hotel Roosevelt in New York, that's how cheap a league we were) and hoping to find finality. We found finality in Toronto where Stavro was interested, courteous but cautious. No, he said. So, we moved on.

We found great enthusiasm in DC and a commitment: We will join. But only if Rochester comes, too. And only if you, meaning me, will do the PA announcing for us at the first game. I would have sung the national anthems of every country in the UN if it meant keeping the league alive, so that part was easy to agree with, though I could never fathom what good it would do. The other part was not so easy.

It came down to convincing Pat Dinolfo and Charlie Schiano, the Rochester owners. If they made it five, Washington would make it six and we were in business for 1970 and so we had a League meeting in the shadows of the O'Hare Expressway and tried to get Pat and Charlie to join and pay the franchise fee. They said they would join but, as we needed them as much as they wanted in, they would not pay. We stood firm and the anxious times began. Pat and Charlie left the room, swearing not to pay. We let them leave the room, swearing that they must pay.

Panic. If we let them go, we were doomed. Would they crack and return? Would we have to rush out, casually of course, before they left the motel? We talked. We worried. We were on the first floor, looking out in the dog-leg of the motel forecourt, so we pulled back the drapes a fraction, to make sure they were not outside the motel waiting for a taxi. And they were outside wondering, too, whether to come back in or wait to see if we would follow them out. It was nerve-racking, with nobody sure what to do. Who gave in? I honestly didn't remember but Charlie Schiano did and he must be right:

"The League gave in," says Charlie. "First of all, Ted Martin, from St. Louis, said the franchise fee was $25,000. Then it came down to $15,000, to $10,000, then $5,000 and we said we had already paid a franchise fee to the ASL (we didn't say it was only $500) and we were not going to pay another one. So, we left and I was pulling Pat away and he was pulling me back and you guys were looking through the gaps in the drapes to see if we were leaving and someone fetched us back in and that was that. What you didn't know was that we were under tremendous pressure from Bill Cox to stay in the ASL because then, he argued, the NASL would fold and the clubs would have to come into the ASL." So they were in. So was Washington. We were six.

FROM AN UNDERGROUND
PARKING LOT IN MEXICO CITY . . .
THE WORLD CUP!

THIS IS THE day I almost quit and ended my part of the tale right here. It happened because of John Smith, once an executive of the London club Queen's Park Rangers and then an executive, in 1967 and 1968, with the New York Generals and now, in 1970, an executive with Leicester City, in the old English First Division.

John, like myself, felt there was a better way for English clubs to be run, more open, more PR and marketing oriented and he felt I could do a job for Leicester. He persuaded the then chairman, Len Shipman, who was also Chairman of the Football League to fly me over for an interview and, intrigued, I went. I made a lengthy presentation to Shipman and his board and when we walked out John said "you've got the job, for sure." Oh, I said, how can you be sure? "Because they didn't understand a word you said."

In a way I knew what he meant from a capsule in my mind from previous years when I was once covering a Leicester City game. I happened to be in the then-secretary's office before the game when a steward came and said that Charlie or Fred or Bill, obviously a known fan, was complaining that the men's toilets were overflowing. The response was a simple: Tell him he's come to see a football match. If he wanted a leak, he should have stayed at home.

How, I pondered, could that attitude even comprehend my talk of community relations and PR and promotions and season ticket holder benefits and player appearances and whatnot? Perhaps the contrast between the American way of openness, contact with the media and the public, and the English way of those times (the game starts at 3, you should know that, and if you want to come, come; if not, stay away) can be better understood through the feelings of so many players who came from one to the other.

Some took to it like a duck to water, this attitude, and this need, to not just be approachable but to approach first. As I used to put it, if we don't go to visit them first, we can't expect them to come and visit us. Ron Newman was one of those irrepressible ones who leapt at the opportunity, as early as his first days as a player with the Atlanta Chiefs when a ceremonial welcoming bus tour was being welcomed by the locals with not much more enthusiasm than their forebears welcomed Sherman a century before. So, Ron hopped off the bus, with another player and a ball, and started heading it to and fro, giving the folks a show and a laugh.

Cliff Calvert, a player with great speed whose confidence grew in leaps and bounds the longer he spent with the Toronto Blizzard and away from the confining boundaries of Sheffield United, took longer to adjust, reluctant to do what had to be done, what he was commanded to do in terms of public appearances and clinics and such, until one day coming into the office to say that now he understood it was necessary and how much he was now enjoying it all.

Vince Casey, speaking of his days as PR man for the New England Tea Men, had to introduce the idea of the positive approach to players whose contact with the media back home, as I was fully aware from my reporting days, was mainly limited to brief, sometimes furtive exchanges in the stadium parking lot as they walked, usually fast, towards their cars and away. Said Vince: "I think they actually looked forward to it. It was fresh and new to them; none of the suspicion they had with the British press." Derek Smethurst, the Tampa Bay striker, is another one who took to it all too slowly, not liking the grind of school visit after school visit, but suddenly delighted with the appearance of soccer balls everywhere, on fields that had not seen them before and finally coming to the conclusion that it was good for the game and good for him, too.

In case there is any misunderstanding, this was not a case of sending players out into the communities in haphazard fashion. No, to greater or lesser extents, there was a clearly defined program of school visits, youth group visits, community organization speech giving, skill demonstrations at fairs and rallies and lessons on how to behave and what to do and what to say before going out. Even in the days of Pele and Beckenbauer (at least, when I was still President of the Cosmos), we took a bus to a school somewhere in the region at least once a week to hold a normal training session in front of the entire assembled school body, plus parents, friends and anyone who had heard we were coming. Of course, we would have a ticket booth set up, too. On the theory I mentioned before . . . we have come to visit you, here's your chance to visit us.

So, with all those differences of how to run a club in mind, I waited to see what Leicester would say. Well, the job offer came and I quit and Lamar Hunt and Phil Woosnam didn't want me to go, so Lamar wrote to Len Shipman saying how important I was to the cause and could they hold the job open until September, to see if we had a league or not? Len Shipman agreed; in September we had a league and New York beckoned, so I stayed.

It does make one wonder how fate plays out. I know I would have made a positive impact at Leicester and if the offer had come from a London team instead of semirural Leicester, not unlike a larger Exeter where I grew up, I think I would have taken it. Who knows what might have happened. Had I gone, though, there would have been no Cosmos, because that was the name I invented, and no Pele or Beckenbauer, you can be sure.

Al Miller, the first truly good American coach, who rose from Hartwick College in upstate New York through the Phildelphia Atoms, where he won the championship, and on through other clubs to coach the US national team, and truly, deeply American, would not have written congratulating me on my US citizenship in 1977.

(I would not have spent hours filling in the citizen application, either, where it says list all your departures and returns since you arrived in the country. As this was post-Pele, that accounting took many, many pages, so when in for the final interview, the immigration official picked up my file, opened it and said: Oh, it's you!)

Likewise our daughter Gaynor would not have presented us with the perfect grandson in Cameron; nor, given the limited sunshine and plentiful gloomy days of England, is she likely to have contracted melanoma and died at the early age of 46; nor would son Robert have been commissioned into the US Marine Corps and later present us with another bundle of energy, granddaughter Natalie and two years later another grandson in Daniel—and the most magnificent Yorkshire terrier ever born, Zamis, Lord of Ilkley Moor, to give him his pedigree name, would have been living with someone else and giving them the knowing, demanding looks he gave us for 16 years and more. Which reminds me that generally, I much prefer animals to humans. After all, from the way the human race carries on, we're the ultimate Weapons of Mass Destruction.

It was about this time, the time of Rochester's entry, that another great debate began over whose rules we would follow—the Laws of the Game, as they are grandly called, first drafted in 1863 in a pub, The Freemasons Arms, in Covent Garden, London and still recognizable today from those drafted when the American Civil War was in full flow? Or whatever alteration came to the mind of someone in the NASL and could be rushed through a league meeting? So, whose rules? Charlie Schiano and Pat Dinolfo—Charlie much more than Pat—were part of the three-ring circus which followed us for many years over how the game should be played.

If motherhood, the flag and apple pie are American, then so is changing the rules and while we changed some rules, how hard we had to fight not to change all of them. Charlie, I recall, suggested a couple of good ones; good in the sense that they bring a chuckle even after all these years. One was to have unlimited substitution and resubstitution so that, for instance, when you had a corner kick you could bring on your 6-foot, 4-inch heading specialist. Yes but then the defense brings on their 6-foot, 5-inch heading specialist, Charlie, and then where are you?

So that one never got anywhere, though then there was the idea of not only bigger goals (on the theory that when the goal size was established way back when, normal men might be 5-foot 8 or so, not the 6-foot plus that most goalkeepers now were) but of bigger goalposts; wider ones so that the ball would hit them more, instead of whizzing by, and thus there would be more rebounds and goalmouth action and people would not complain so much about near misses. Yes, but what about all the near misses that are bound to happen just past the wider posts and still not satisfy everyone? So that one bit the dust, too.

Charlie was present at the end of one great experiment on September 1, 1972, when the Rochester Lancers played the Dallas Tornado in the first game of a three-game playoff series. As we tried any which way to avoid drawn games, we were then playing successive 15 minutes of extra time until someone scored the winning goal and on this night, our efforts led to The Longest Game, 15-minute overtime after 15-minute overtime; 176 minutes in all, just four minutes short of two full games, for heaven's sake, when the winner from Carlos Metidieri trickled over the line. Ron Newman, then Dallas coach, was there to recall: "I remember it well. It was the only game that I ever remember where both teams celebrated the winning goal.

"I think Phil was on the way down from the press box to call the game as neither team could run anymore. The press box was just a slab with chairs on it as it had burned down a few days earlier. Kenny Cooper played in goal, even though he had not recovered sufficiently from a knee operation. Kenny was a real hero as he hopped about the goalmouth for four hours. Our other goalkeeper—Mirko Stojanovic had been suspended by me for disciplinary reason."

"Mirko apologized after the game for his actions and played magnificently in going on to win the championship. The game rightfully made the Guinness book of records and then later taken out but I never found out why."

Charlie Schiano claimed it was his idea, to play to a finish. "I was fed up with those tied games. Peter Short, who was so sadly shot and killed in a robbery in Los Angeles later, said to me before the game: "But, Charlie, we could be here all night." And I said don't worry, Peter, someone will score a goal. Well, when we got to the fourth overtime period, he looked up at me from the bench and we made eye contact and he didn't say a word. Just the look, that was enough. Lamar Hunt and Bill McNutt were there with Dallas and Lamar said "shall we call the game, we'll be here all night?" and I said no problem, we'll arrange breakfast." Charlie was by no means the worst offender; at least he made his suggestions with humor and accepted his defeats the same way.

Not so, the humor along with ideas, from some of the other owners, despite the fact that we did make changes and that got us in hot water with, on the one side, owners who wanted more and with FIFA on the other, who wanted none. Bob Bell, owner of San Diego, thought about it this way: "We need major changes in the structure of the game but we can't make them because of FIFA. Every sport makes changes to improve its product. We can't do it and that's a serious problem."

FIFA general secretary Dr. Helmut Kaser suggested we were ignoring the beauty of the game and doing it only for profit. FIFA, of course, under the Presidency of Joao Havelange and his successor, Dr. K's own ex-son-in-law Sepp Blatter, or as I prefer to call him, Septic Bladder, was never interested in money. Not at all. Of course. Their motto says For the Good of the Game, doesn't it?. Filthy lucre doesn't come into it, naturally. Money? Tosh, pish, get thee behind me Satan. I mean, if a used car dealer changes his company name from Bob Smith to Honest Bob Smith, would suspicions not enter your mind? Thus FIFA always stood for the good of the game. By adding that line to the logo, methinks they protest too much.

At least Dr. K was basically a decent old stick, with a lovely old dog always lolling by his desk, and he didn't live long enough to see what FIFA was to become and how they finally came out of the closet with a headline splashed across the cover of their own house publication, FIFA Magazine, in June 2003: The billion dollar business. Silly us, we thought it was sport.

It got so bad in 1981 that FIFA was about to banish us all for life, if not longer, when we tried to get a meeting with them to explain and implore which is where Noel Lemon came in and the Fight of the Century took place.

No, Noel was not in that fight. Everyone who knows Noel recognizes his sweet temperament, his lack of instant, aggressive reaction, his quiet acceptance of defeat and other forms of torture. How the *Tulsa Tribune* could write a long feature story about him and headline it "Sour Lemon" is a mystery. (Exploding Orange, might have been a better one, considering Noel's Ulster origins and temperament.)

But, no, this is where Noel was the peacemaker and the salvation of our problems, if only people had listened. As I said, Noel is from Northern Ireland and at the time the Senior Vice President of FIFA was Harry Cavan, a nice old chap and, roll of drums, from Northern Ireland. So, first of all Noel pulled the magic trick of getting FIFA to agree to let us meet their Executive Committee, meeting at the Ritz Hotel, in Madrid. That may not sound like magic but it was because FIFA deals only with other national associations, not with leagues and this was the first time—and last so far—that they condescended to meet with the likes of us.

Off we trotted to Madrid, with Noel and Kurt Lamm and Gene Edwards, the USSF President, Phil Woosnam and Lee Stern of Chicago, the NASL Executive Committee Chairman of the time and the night before the meeting, off upstairs trotted Noel to meet Harry and came down with the deal done. We could carry on with our rule changes for the rest of the season, and this was still springtime and almost all the season to go and then would have to cease and desist the next year. Springtime, mind you, with the season already begun and we did not know, from game to game, what rules we would be playing with. Boggles the mind? I think we could have made the change at half time and no one would have worried; the N in NASL did not stand for Normality.

Next morning, FIFA allowed only Edwards and Stern into the room and after a while they came out looking daggers at each other and beginning to argue. Now let me paint the scene. I was standing at the corner of a lush, plush corridor outside the meeting room in the most elegant hotel in Madrid, itself as elegant a city as any in the world, one leg of the wide corridor going away to my left and another going away to the right and only from my vantage point could you see left and right.

On my left, the President of the Federation and the Chairman of the League are now engaged in some pushing and shoving, which soon becomes a punch here and a punch there and a general free for all as Noel and others try to separate them. On my right, advancing at a steady pace towards us, is a significant-sized sample of the world's football media, wanting to get the story of our good or ill fate at the hands of FIFA. They almost got a story they had not bargained on getting, the Fight of the Century.

Happily, with pushing and pulling and quiet but terse and threatening orders to behave themselves, they stopped and straightened ties and smoothed ruffled hair and managed, just, to look the part of responsible executives as the media corps coalesced around us.

But what had we actually done to change the game and perturb the lords of FIFA? We had given players a number to wear all season, so the fans could identify them, because in those days #1 was a goalkeeper, #2 the right back, #3 the left back and so on until #11 the outside left. If you did not know them on sight, then you didn't know them. This is, of course, now common practice.

We put the players' names on the back of their shirts. This is now common practice. We troubled over the game-killing back-passing to the goalkeeper. The goalkeeper is now not allowed to handle a back pass. We allowed three substitutions, instead of the FIFA-mandated two. Three substitutes are now permitted.

We had the shoot-out, as a means of settling a drawn game, instead of penalty kicks. This was more like a part of the game, where the player had

10 seconds, starting at the 35-yard line, to try to score and the goalkeeper could do whatever he liked. You know, like in a real part of the game. The fans loved it.

But, oh, that 35-yard line! That is where offside could be called, not at the half-way line, and thus defenses could not push up so far and thus there was more room in the middle of the field and thus skilled players had more time to show their skills and please the fans. Isn't that a good idea, to please the fans? Obviously not. From FIFA's reaction, you would have thought that all the things we tried fell just short of murdering the game.

It is just coincidence that Charlie Schiano and the Rochester Lancers were part of another experiment, too, our early introduction into international competition, when we entered them, as our champions, in the CONCACAF Clubs' championship. They won the first round home and away games against a team from Panama and then waited for the second round draw and pairings. And waited. And waited. And waited. Finally, the news reached the league office and Rochester with orders to play their home game against a Mexican team in February. In Rochester, in February when the snow has been coming off Lake Ontario for weeks and you enter the outdoors in nothing less than the warmest clothes money can buy and the field at Aquinas Stadium, the field anywhere for that matter, would be several feet under. It did not help convince skeptical owners that we really did need to be a part of soccer and not apart from soccer.

Even so, says Charlie: "The whole thing was still a big step-up for us from the ASL. We played the Boston Astros this one year and had a hard time finding the field because they couldn't pay their bills and no one would let them back again. So this time, they're playing at Chesterfield and the owner John Bertos is out there selling the tickets and his wife is cooking the hot dogs. A week or so later, they were short of players and John Bertos played in goal. We also played at Eintracht Oval in Queens, oh boy. The locker room was in a cellar under a bar and the only way in was through the fire escape at the back of the bar and down spiral stairs into the cellar. I told Enzo Magnozzi, their owner, that we wanted a phone line and an electrical outlet so we could broadcast the game on radio and he said why broadcast it, what's the point? And we said, well we're trying to make our sport and team popular. He didn't understand what we were talking about. Ten years later, we're playing the Cosmos in front of 73,000 people at Giants Stadium."

But some things at Rochester never changed. Dick Howard, goalkeeper for Toronto and the Lancers and later an important coaching instructor and committee chairman for the Canadian Soccer Association and CON-CACAF, speaks of the days when: "Match officials involved in Lancer games at Aquinas Stadium were often concerned about their well being especially if calls had been made against the hometown team during the game . . . the final whistle was made when the ball was located at the open end of the stadium.. so that all the officials could sprint to a waiting car for a fast exit to the airport before the fans could realize what had happened! (Yours truly also felt like doing the same thing if a bad goal had been conceded!!!)."

Mike Lewis, reporter then in Rochester and later for the New York *Daily News,* recalls similar dangers: "Don Popovic, the coach, had done something wrong, again, swearing at the referee maybe and was banned by the League from sitting on the bench. So, he got a ladder and climbed up onto the top of the roof, phoning his comments down to Charlie on the bench. Well, things weren't going well and the fans started booing and looking angry and Charlie decided a police escort was needed—not to get Don out of the stadium, just down off the roof."

At this point, it may be thought by a neutral observer that Rochester, New York figures large in the less than respectful parts of this tome. Well, yes, that is true. After all, the NASL talked about introducing a contest where the third place winners won a two-week trip to Rochester; the second place winners won a one-week trip to Rochester and the outright winners didn't have to go at all. Then there was the inestimable John Petrossi.

Jack Daley, who progressed from public relations in Toronto to become one of the most successful general managers when he moved west to Seattle and the Sounders, remembers the Petrossi Principle better than I. Jack recalled: "Four new clubs came on board in 1973, from Vancouver, Seattle, San Jose and Los Angeles. With expansion came increased operating costs, especially in the team travel department. Where a one-day trip in the same time zone used to be the norm, teams were now looking at cross-country trips of several days.

"So, to help with the mounting costs Pat and Charlie offered partial ownership to John Petrossi, who owned a cement production business and was known to be a bottom-line operator. In addition to providing a new infusion of cash, Petrossi took over the business operations of the Lancers. He came to the League meeting before the 1974 season and made the eloquent point that each club seemed to generate a decent home gate but that was washed out by all the travel costs.

"He therefore proposed that each team play 20 games at home and only 12 on the road for a 32-game schedule. He argued that the increase in home games would generate sufficient revenue to cover the now reduced road schedule. Ted Howard, who was responsible for all the scheduling, politely informed Petrossi that a 20-home, 12-away game schedule was physically impossible. Angered at the mathematical logic coming from Ted, Petrossi stormed: 'What do you mean, you can't play 20 home and 12 on the road. You guys in the League office work it out.' He never attended a League meeting again!" My own counter proposal to John was that the league signed 30 players in total and bussed them around, with different names and shirts, to represent all the clubs in turn. I think he would have liked that idea.

For contrast to our sometime circus, 1970 was the year of the World Cup in Mexico, the World Cup of Brazil beating Italy in the final, of Gordon Banks one-handed save from Pele that ranks as probably the greatest save ever made, of Carlos Alberto holding the World Cup aloft (and there's three players later destined for the NASL).

The only places where you could watch the World Cup of 1970 was by closed circuit in Madison Square Garden and the Forum in Los Angeles, rights purchased by the NASL for a very few thousand dollars. Nobody else wanted it. Nobody else was available to do the play-by-play or the expert commentary, at least not for nothing, so I was elected and trotted off to Mexico City to get my credentials and broadcast position. The Mexican TV people could not have been more courteous; handed over my credential and escorted me to the elevator to go down to the parking garage. Off to Azteca, I thought, and a car to take me there; what service.

I found it strange that the parking level we entered was absolutely empty of cars; empty of everything except this strange looking box in the middle which, as we approached, turned out to be a room made out of empty egg cartons, with one door, through which we entered to find a TV set, a chair, a microphone and my broadcast position. The USA rights holders in those days did not warrant a seat at Azteca. Not that it mattered. We realized after one game that a confined closed-circuit audience makes as much noise as that in a stadium and they couldn't hear a word I said. So I did the rest of the games from the comfort of the Univision office on Park Avenue, confining my output to giving the line-ups before the game, and the noise, began and summarizing at half time and the end. Saved the long trip and expense to Mexico City and sometimes I was home in time for dinner.

Nor did the USA get a place in the finals. Two victories over Bermuda and one over Canada were not enough to compensate for losing once to Canada and twice to Haiti. Not that many noticed that either. The NASL (that is, Phil Woosnam and myself) promoted the home games against Bermuda and Canada in Atlanta and Kansas City and had trouble to get people to attend . . . and even more trouble in getting people to understand what a national team was; a weird thought it certainly was for people accustomed only to domestic, isolationist sport in those days. But we did come up with a slogan—Soccer: The Sport of the Seventies.

Before I move on from Mexico, I must tell a story of my first visit there in 1962. I was in Lima, Peru for Peru vs England, on the way to the World Cup in Chile when someone in the sports department of the *Daily Express* in London looked at a map, thought Lima wasn't far from Mexico City, so why don't you nip up there and cover Mexico vs Wales while you're about it?

This was all in medieval times, in terms of transport and communication, you understand. Lima to Mexico City was, first, a long haul by prop plane to Panama, overnight in Panama City and then hopping on an airline no longer in business, Panagra, through every capital city, and some others, in Central America before reaching Mexico City. Interesting experience, incidentally in Guatemala. If you were actually landing to enter that country, you lined up for a thorough inspection of documents, body and luggage by a series of groups of armed men. If you were in transit, you entered a large room, the far wall of which had this huge gap in it, where maybe a vast door had once stood, and through which you now sauntered, unhindered, into Guatemala; which I did, to buy a few souvenirs and have a shoe shine. If I had hurried, I could have nipped downtown, assassinated the President and been back in time to journey onward.

Communication was equally Neanderthal. International phone calls were either impossible or very difficult (even from the US to the UK you had to dial O, then ask for Operator White Plains 90, give your number and the number you were calling, hang up and wait for 5, 10, 20, 30 minutes). From most countries it was impossible and thus you carried a Cable and Wireless Credit Card and, having typed your story on your ubiquitous portable typewriter, handed it to a Cable and Wireless teleprinter operator, either in the company office or at the stadium and he sent it on its way.

The *Daily Express,* having decided to send me up to the Wales game, decided to make the most of it by arranging to plaster Wales with billboards, making arrangements to do a special edition and fly it down to Wales at dawn, the game ending at about 4 a.m., UK time, so all of Wales could read about it in our paper alone. That, and scores of examples like it, is why we sold 4.5 million copies a day back then. So, arriving in Mexico City on the morning of the game, I went to the Cable and Wireless Office to make arrangements to file my story. Ah, sorry, Senor, they said, we can not accept your credit card without permission of the Ministry of Something Or Other. Leaving aside oaths and protestations, I asked where that office was located and was given the address where, when found, another polite person told me it wasn't going to be open again until the morning, the morning after the game.

So, frustrated at all turns, I went back to the Cable and Wireless office and paid for and sent a brief message: Regret cannot file, credit card refused. At least, I thought, they can stand down the overtime staff, tell the pilot to switch off the propellers and go home. The Wales manager Jimmy Murphy said that as I wasn't working, I might as well join him on the bench and after the game I was sitting in the team bus when this man stepped into the well of the bus and called out my name.

Here, I said. "Ah Senor Toye, everything is now all right, we can accept your credit card." Sod it, I thought, but said to the man from Cable and Wireless that while I thanked him, it didn't matter any more because it was much too late and in any case I had sent a message to the office saying not to expect a story from me. At which he beamed and said: "But do not worry, Senor. We did not send that message."

I was fortunate to be on a midnight plane that night, via Lima to Santiago de Chile with the Mexican team, and therefore not reachable during the immediate period when the London office was ready to boil me in oil, carve up little pieces and recall me. And then fire me. I filed a factual piece from Lima airport and hurried back on the plane before a return recall message could arrive.

Hmmm, well, just one more that has nothing to do with the NASL but to show how we have progressed towards instant communications to any-where, from anywhere, before I continue. Birmingham City were kicking their way through the First Division and Europe in 1960, the Brummie Bashers they were named, and on a few hours notice I was on the way to report their game in Seville, Spain. There, arriving the morning of the game, I tried all the normal channels to get a telephone in the stadium without success and finally turned to the British Consul there for help. He worked a seeming miracle and I was provided with the actual number of the telephone I would have that night so that the office could book a series of calls to me there, because calling out would be impossible.

Early at the stadium, I went up to the press level, found my seat loca-tion, found the telephone on the shelf, compared numbers and found it was the right one and settled down for the first booked call to come thru 15 minutes before the kick off. It didn't come. Nor the next. Nor the next. So I thought I had better follow the phone lines, see if there was a wire loose or even someone didn't plug it in. Which is, in fact, what had hap-pened. It was not plugged in because there was no plug, no line connect-ing the press box to the outside world, nothing. I had wanted a phone, with a number, and had used undue influence to get a phone with a num-ber. And that's what I had been given, a phone with a number.

Mexico, though, was where a chance meeting took place at one of those boundless receptions in the many elegant watering holes of that nation's capital which led, as we shall soon see, to the beginnings of a different life.

If one of the most famous clubs in the world was yet to be born and named or was, indeed, yet to be conceived, Mexico City, it could be said, is where the first looks and words of courtship were to be exchanged.

IT'S THE COSMOS.
WHO? SAID PELE

THE NEW YORK pro sports franchise which came into being immediately before the Cosmos was the New York Mets and that's how the Cosmos got their name.

Mets is short for Metropolitan and I wanted something bigger and better than mere Metropolitan and, running through all the words I could come up with, came up with Cosmopolitan. Hmm. That's about right for New York, that's about right for soccer but Cosmopolitans? Cosmopolites? So what about shortening it to Cosmos, then? Perfect. At least, I thought so. Nesuhi Ertegun, with his background in music, wanted to call us the Blues. Someone else suggested pink uniforms and hearts along the edges and calling us the New York Lovers, ensuring us of much attention, so he thought.

With Pele in mind, I chose the colors of Brazil and ran a competition (two free tickets to Zurich, courtesy of Swissair) and waited for the entries to come in, discarding them all (well, amounting to fewer than 40 all told) until I came to one from two schoolteachers in Queens. Cosmos, they said, so with a genuine winner in hand, I could manufacture several other Cosmos entries and declare it the people's choice. Well, mine anyway. Wayland Moore, an excellent artist in Atlanta whom some called the Leroy Neimann of the South, did the logo for me for $250 and a famous logo for a famous club was born.

How we, Phil Woosnam and I, got the owners for the franchise that became the Cosmos is another deviating story. We knew, from our eyrie on Peachtree Street that we needed someone, or someones, out of the ordinary and the first person we tried was Sir David Frost, a notable, even famous English TV personality who was then very well known in the

USA and with whom I had appeared on numerous BBC talk shows and panels about football, so I wrote to him.

We had a reply, and then a meeting with his New York lawyer, a very helpful man, who said that this was not something that David could undertake and why didn't we try Nesuhi Ertegun. Who? Nesuhi Ertegun, Turkish, a football fanatic, from a family of distinction whose father had been Ambassador to the Court of St James (i.e. Britain) and the USA and was now truly among the major players in the record industry along with his brother Ahmet. Trying to penetrate such a level of the entertainment world's high and mighty was well nigh beyond us but by complete chance Phil had met Nesuhi at a reception during the World Cup in Mexico in 1970 and eventually Nesuhi led us to a company called National Kinney, once a funeral home and limousine company turned into a major parking lot operator and now being conglomerated, if there is such a word, into Warner Communications by a man named Steve Ross.

Phil came back very excited from his first meeting with Steve. A very powerful man, he said, and indeed he was, and committed in no time at all. So Steve Ross, Nesuhi and Ahmet and Jay Emmett, whose Licensing Corporation of America had been brought into the fold, and Ted Ashley, head of Warner Bros and Alan Cohen and four other executives bought into the idea and owned it for the first year at which point it was sold, gladly, probably, because we had lost all their money, to the corporation itself.

But who was going to run the Cosmos? That's a question I almost gloss over because Phil and I had long ago decided that he would run the league and I would run the most important franchise, in New York, whenever it came about. Unless the owners really wanted Phil and then we'd reverse roles. All we had to do was to let them know the fate we had determined for them, right? It must seem somewhat outrageous now, the absolute overwhelming certainty with which we approached those, and other matters, but it must have worked because that's what I became, Vice President and General Manager. Of course, it may have been that no one else wanted the job.

It did not take long to sign the first Cosmos team in 1971. As you enter JFK Airport from the Van Wyck Expressway, there is a large hotel off to the right. It has gone through many owners and many names and I forget what it was called that Sunday afternoon in March, 1971, when we signed all the players, in one afternoon, for $75 a game. Take it or leave it. Gordon Bradley did most of the work. I had hired him as coach in preference to the only other real candidate, Alkis Panagoulias, who later was the Greek national coach when they qualified for the 1994 World Cup in the USA.

Gordon, from Sunderland by way of Carlisle and Toronto, was coaching and playing in the local German American League for New York Hota. He had played for the New York Generals in 1968 and had, in fact, marked Pele out of the game in a Generals-Santos exhibition game. Alkis was coach of the New York Greek Americans. Both knew the local players and local players were going to be the first Cosmos players.

So after looking, talking and analyzing, we called the chosen few to the hotel at JFK and had a team. Jorge Siega was the first Cosmos player, an outside left from Brazil, long a resident in New York and playing for the German-Hungarians. Jorge had a great left foot, always seeming to be able to extend just that far enough from the defender closing in and get his cross over . . . where often it was met by the Honorable KHR Horton, Minister of the Crown Colony of Bermuda, a very distinguished looking gentleman now, superbly groomed, but back in those old days just plain Randy Horton, a large, ungainly man, fully 6 feet, 6 inches, of which several inches were his Afro, which matched his full beard and made him look a menace. Which he was, to most opposing defenses. Randy was then studying at Rutgers University in New Jersey and had a round-trip drive of about five hours to get to practice at nights. All for $75 a game. We were now two months old, from the time I opened shop (in two rooms at the Hotel Roosevelt, near Grand Central Station, with Pauline Badal, a secretary borrowed from one of the Warner executives) in January 1971 when we had no name, no coach, no stadium, no players. But even before we signed our first players, I had been to talk to one of our future players.

In February '71, Santos were playing in a friendly game in Kingston, Jamaica, so Phil Woosnam, Kurt Lamm, then General Secretary of the USSFA and I went down to tell Pele he was wanted in New York one day.

We met him, with Julio Mazzei, his constant companion in attendance, by the side of the pool at the Sheraton Hotel and told him our tale; that soccer was in its infancy in the USA, that the time would come when he would be ready to depart Santos and Brazil for a fresh challenge, that he and he alone could create the media attention, inspire the youth, draw the crowds, that New York was the place, the only place, to do it and, in return, he would earn more adulation and gratitude than he could imagine. He was courteous, of course, and Pele was always courteous but, as he admitted afterwards, his thoughts were—Why are they telling me this? What has New York to do with me? He went his way and we went ours, in my case back to the club that had to play its first game at St Louis in April. We won that first game 2–1. And Pele was certainly going to find out the answer to his questions in time. In time after time after time, in fact.

But another World Cup hero from the past was to intrude upon us before 1971 was much older. Suppose Ronaldo, say, or David Beckham scores the winning goal in a momentous World Cup game and then disappears. Do you think we wouldn't have all police forces in the world out looking for him? Well, Joe Gaetjens scored the winning goal in a momentous World Cup game and then disappeared and until his family came to see me in 1971, no one, except for the family, had bothered to look. If you don't know the name Joe Gaetjens, shame on you.

He scored the goal by which the United States beat England at Belo Horizonte, in the 1950 World Cup, and that is still the biggest shocker in the history of the competition; even bigger than the North Korean win over Italy in 1966. (The assist, by the way, was from Walter Bahr, later the noted coach of Penn State and father of a trio of soccer-playing sons who then found more lucrative employment kicking a few times a game in the National Football League. "If it been anyone other than Joe, it might have been a fluke," said Walter "but that was the kind of goal Joe scored"). And when the wire service stories first arrived in newspaper offices around the world, there being no televised games then, the general belief was that a digit had been left out in transmission, it had to be 10–1 to England, didn't it? Well, it wasn't and not long afterwards, Joe disappeared.

His family—his wife (or widow, no one was sure at that time) Lylian and two brothers, one, Gerard, a professor at the University of New Hampshire, the other, Jean Pierre, a successful businessman in Marietta, Georgia—came to see me and asked for help in finding out what had happened to him. What an intriguing story it was and how tragic the truth. Joe was at Columbia University, working in a German restaurant and playing in the local German-American League when he got the call to the national team, a call which never should have been made because he was not then and never became a US citizen. But, then, who knew he was going to be famous?

So he scored the goal, returned to the US, then went to France to play for Racing Club, Paris—and played a lot more around Montmartre and Pigalle, which had him transferred to a Second Division team—and then returned to his homeland in Haiti. There to vanish. We held a press conference; we appealed to the Organization of American States; we tried every which way to get an answer and it finally came.

He had been arrested by the Ton Ton Macoute, Papa Doc Duvalier's thugs, and taken to Port au Prince's notorious jail because his brothers were anti-Duvalier pro-democracy advocates (while Joe himself was totally nonpolitical) and because the Ton Ton Macoute section chief coveted Joe's dry cleaning business. The answer to whether he was still in jail or dead came some time later when a prisoner who had been in jail with Joe told this story: A lot of prisoners were taken out to another jail. All those remaining in Port au Prince jail were executed. Joe was one of those left behind. So his likely date of execution was July 11 or 12, 1967. Just when we were all busy with our first season in the USA.

But now we had another season to play as well as Pele to persuade and I decided the next prod would be to retire a player's jersey. Retiring an illustrious player's jersey and number when he has finished an illustrious career with his club is normal, of course. We retired a player's number before he had even thought of signing a contract with us.

The number? 10, of course, Pele's lifelong number, and I gave him his Cosmos #10 shirt for safe-keeping on the field before a Santos exhibition game at Yankee Stadium against Deportivo Cali of Colombia. I told him the whys and the wherefores and I'm sure he didn't have a clue of what I was talking about.

All our players that first year were signed from the German-American League, with clubs like New York Bavarians and German-Hungarians, New York Hota, Blau Weiss Gottschee and last but not least Blue Star, which might give you a clue that most of the Germans who ran the League, men like Harry Saunders, Henry Uhlfelder, Herbie Heilpern and Walter Marburg were Jewish Germans, part of the flight from Nazi Germany.

They played at places like Eintracht Oval, Metropolitan Oval, Schutzenpark and even Gaelic Park, where once the old, bitter Irish-Americans refused to let this foreign (i.e. English) sport of soccer ever to be played; all small, run-down facilities in urban areas, just managing to resist the developers. They all failed to hold out in the end, except historic old Metropolitan Oval, saved and refurbished in the 90s as a memento and a living, active soccer facility. But if their stadia were in the wrong places to survive, their hearts were in the right place. They worked with us to give us the players, they made the multitude of ethnic clubs in their bars and taverns and hideaways gather to listen to me, sometimes at breakfast, lunch and dinner times on the same day so I sometimes felt like that old movie about American package tourists—If Its Tuesday It Must Be Belgium.

They gave us their own people, people the ordinary followers knew, to sell tickets for us, and got a percentage. They even changed their name to the Cosmopolitan League, to be in tune with the Cosmos. At the start, they were given a piece of the Cosmos, later taken away from them, and then their congregation of ethnics groups were overwhelmed by the wave of Italian immigration, who then dominated the New York area local soccer scene until another wave arrived . . . from all the Spanish-speaking countries where soccer is God. I can not see, incidentally, any future wave of such consequence for the culture of the American game; no more food for the football future to be added to this melting pot.

While I was out on this ethnic lecture circuit, Gordon Bradley was beginning the courtship of American parents and American youth with his overwhelming enthusiasm, his endless giving of clinics and speeches and encouragement. There must be little kids running around with soccer balls today with no idea that until their grandfathers heard Gordon, there wasn't any soccer played where they play all the time.

Mind you, with all those speeches, I never got the kind of reception I received in Toronto, many years later. There was a sizeable core of fanatical Portuguese fans there, mostly Benfica fans who had their own dining, drinking, soccer-watching-and-talking home, Benfica House. So, to try to get them to pay attention to a team a little closer than Lisbon, I got myself invited to make a speech at their annual dinner.

They were not, repeat not, interested, so I told them that I, too, was a Benfiquista—the name the fans call themselves—and had seen Benfica long before many of them, indeed back as far as 1963 with that great team . . . in goal Costa Perreira (ah, what's this, they're looking at me), Cavem and Germano and Jaime Graca and Mario Coluna and (by now, there is some noise, not quite cheering, but rumbling, the stamping of feet, noise) and so on to Eusebio and Torres and by the time I got to number 11, the outside left Simoes, they were all on their feet cheering madly and then clustering round to shake my hand and pat me on the back. I don't think they bought any tickets to see the Blizzard, though.

We eventually moved our office from the Hotel Roosevelt to space on the corner of 101 Park Avenue, on the second floor, hired John O'Reilly as PR director, Marketing director and director of anything else we could think of, and one day found a crowd of people on the sidewalk beneath us shouting abuse and throwing stones. We may not be very good, I thought, but we aren't that bad. Then I found out that on the floor directly above us was the New York office of the PLO and the group below were from the Jewish Defense League.

Good preparation, in a way, for what came a decade later in Toronto when the Mounties had us clear the Blizzard offices at CNE Stadium in a hurry because of a bomb threat. Innocent again, because the Canadian Soccer Association had prohibited a game involving Red Star Belgrade, a Serbian favorite, and in a previous incarnation, the Blizzard had been the Metros-Croatia; so it had to be our fault, hadn't it? The deadly Balkan stew of hate. which ended in mutual attempts at genocide in what was then Yugoslavia, was just simmering.

Actually, we were not bad at all. We reached the playoffs, often pleasing crowds that rose to the giddy heights of four or five thousand, then losing to Atlanta who went on to lose the final to the Dallas Tornado of Lamar Hunt, though goodness knows how Dallas had the legs for it, having just played in that Rochester marathon.

But, for a moment, it didn't matter to me because I quit. I had another very interesting job offer from London so I quit and Jay Emmett asked me "have we done anything wrong?" and I said no, but . . . and I ended up with a better deal and went to my farewell party that same night (my, my, I do have the strangest farewell parties) and walked in to tell them all that I wasn't going after all.

THE TITLE, THE RUSSIANS, AND HOW DIETER LOST HIS HEAD

WE DID OUR bit to warm up the Cold War in 1972 when I brought Moscow Dynamo on a tour, which included a game against us at Hofstra Stadium and others in Atlanta, Dallas and Vancouver. There was a definite Cold War frost in the air when we met them at JFK, cold and formal as we greeted the President, Lev Daryugin and the manager, the great, incomparable goalkeeper Lev Yashin.

There was a little thaw when we took them on the Circle Line boat ride around Manhattan and some amazement when I took the two Levs out to Scarsdale and showed them around, stopping at a local supermarket, where the array of goods astonished them. Who is allowed to shop here, they asked, with knowledge of their own forbidding system of privilege? Anyone, I answered. And had to take them to two other supermarkets to let them see that all manner of people were helping themselves from the shelves.

That may seem a strange thing to say to those who never went behind the Iron Curtain in those simpler days when we all knew where the enemy lived . . . the enemy and millions of people to whom the merest, cheapest morsel of western goods was like a rare and dazzling gift.

Example. I was in Bratislava (then part of Czechoslovakia, now capital of Slovakia) for a Slovan Bratislava vs Tottenham Hotspur game and was standing on the touchline of their dimly lit stadium (in their very dimly lit city) the evening before the game when this man approached and introduced himself as the Slovan captain. Would I like to see the field? he asked. Thanks, but I can see it from here, said I, as I was about a yard from the touchline. No, no, he said, please come and see what it looks like out there, pointing to the middle. So, not to be rude, I walked out with him to the center circle at which point he came to the point.

Now we were out of earshot of any possible listening device, he said he wanted to strike a bargain. If he gave me a set of glasses of the local, and superb, crystal, would I give him an equal amount of cosmetic and such when he came to London for the second leg in two weeks' time? As I didn't think the captain of Slovan was likely to be in the Secret Police, I agreed and gave him armfuls stuff from Woolworths, his chosen store, when he came to London. We still have a few of those beautiful crystal glasses.

Another example. All the Iron Curtain countries had shops where only foreign currency could be spent, often only by foreigners too, and within which were some cheap perfume, a few boxes of chocolates, maybe some nylons and stuff you wouldn't look at twice . . . unless you lived there. Then you might encounter, as did I, the pitiful sight of an official of the local pro club or national association, standing outside with his nose pressed to the glass, trying to direct you to the goods he wanted you to buy for him with the few pounds or dollars he had managed to accumulate over the years . . . to which, out of sheer embarrassment, you would add a few of your own without letting him see.

Well, after the two Levs had finally grasped that freedom to shop was something we all took for granted, we had a small party at the house and saw the change coming when Daryugin presented me with a cigar . . . which I lit with gusto . . . and had it explode in my face. He'd bought it for me at a Times Square novelty shop. He also brought copious caviar and volumes of vodka which cost me many a late night and painful morning as I accompanied them on part of their tour, retiring in exhaustion as they went west. They came back through New York on the way home, having celebrated all the way from Vancouver and emptying the liquor supply of at least two airlines on the way. There was nothing formal or frosty about their departure, with bear hugs mixing with the fumes and smiles.

Before he died so tragically of cancer, I met Lev Yashin many times on the soccer circuit but one occasion sticks in my mind. It was in a restaurant within sight of the Santiago Bernabeu Stadium, Madrid, the night before it would host the World Cup Final of 1982. There, at this private table were Pele, the Black Pearl; Eusebio of Portugal, the Black Panther; and Yashin. With his limited command of English and my Russian confined to the one word which sounded like Bustarov (and meant Down the Hatch, as another vodka went past the tonsils) he was having a hard time explaining something, pointing at Pele and Eusebio and then himself. Finally, he took a menu and drew on it a spider and then I remembered. Yashin always wore all black; in the nets he looked just like that—a spider—and that was his nickname, the Black Spider. So the Black Pearl, the Black Panther and the Black Spider signed the tablecloth. And Eric King, then secretary of the Canadian Soccer Association, had it off the table and guarded like the crown jewels before you could say Ottawa.

Bringing Moscow Dynamo, mind you, was not just to have a soccer game. I tried, often, to bring a geopolitical aspect to some part of the operation, so that we could grow out of the purely sporting into other pages, other media; break down the early crust of indifference, even antagonism, and get some space. Hence the negotiations, successful later, for the People's Republic of China and Cuba. Israel vs Palestine would be a nice game to be able to stage, one of these days, if such days ever come.

Not that the Dynamo visit was without complications. They were due in the USA in May, flying right after playing Glasgow Rangers in the final of the UEFA (Union of European Football Associations) Cup in Spain. But with Rangers winning 2–0, some of their fans invaded the field in celebration a couple of minutes before the final whistle—and that gave Dynamo the chance to protest the game, demand a replay and not get on the plane. We were moving into our house in Scarsdale that very day and the first phone call I took was from Pauline Badal in the office to tell me the Russians were not traveling. As it happens, FIFA was meeting in Vienna the next day, so I flew that night to Frankfurt, found the only connecting flight booked and strode up and down the line of waiting passengers offered $100 for anyone's boarding pass. (Contemplate: Try doing that in this day of fear and security).

With one in hand, I flew to Vienna and laid my case before the FIFA President Sir Stanley Rous, who it might be appropriate to call the Last Honorable Man in that position, who had attended college in Exeter, where I grew up, and whose ghost writer I had once been. He fumed at the Russian attitude and ordered them to travel at the next suitable time for us, which was in August, and to take less money for all the trouble they had caused.

This led to the beginnings of my doubts about certain standards, or flaws, in American education. I asked someone, whose blushes should be spared as he is probably now a respected member of his community and a revered grandfather, and who had a degree from a well-known university, to set up a conference call with New York, Atlanta, Dallas, Vancouver and Lisbon (where a Dynamo rep would be present). He scribbled the names and when he got to the last, a blank look appeared and he asked: where's that? Where's that! A taxi driver in St. Louis once said to a member of the Toronto Blizzard staff: You come from Canada? Yeah, sure, that's just outside Detroit, isn't it? But I don't think he boasted a degree in journalism from a respected university.

As late as 2005, I found yet another sporting example of the sheer ignorance of the world which abounds in the USA. The US Open Golf championship had just been won by Michael Campbell of New Zealand and Mike Canizzaro of the New York Post wrote that he, Campbell, came from a part of New Zealand called Maori. There is no part of New Zealand called Maori. The Maori are the original inhabitants of New Zealand. So, I e-mailed the Post: If Michael Campbell comes from a part of New Zealand called Maori, then your writer comes from a part of New York called Ignoramus.

Time has changed to a great extent, though, and millions of young Americans have watched soccer games and players from around the world, thousands of them have been around the world; so let us think of soccer as a lesson in geography, and a lesson in people, too.

There is nothing to compare with soccer for the opportunity to meet people, people of all kinds and classes and colors. I have come across absolute stinkers in the land of my birth and the land where I expect I'll be buried and some truly excellent people among Israelis and Arabs, in countries once hostile, like China and Vietnam, countries with appalling reputations, like Colombia and Zimbabwe, and on both sides of the black/white divide in apartheid era South Africa. I am trying hard to find something nice to say about the French.

Both at the start of the Bays and the start of the Cosmos, getting players had been one of the first, obvious and ongoing tasks. But selling a player? Actually getting money for him? That was a new experience and it happened at half time, yes half time, of the championship game between the

Cosmos and St. Louis Stars at Hofstra Stadium. To get from the locker room to the field, the players had to pass through a narrow way with spectators on either side. So as John Kerr, our midfield dynamo, was going out again for the second half, he was stopped and asked: Would you like to play in Mexico? I am from Club America. Well, I have heard of unorthodox approaches, backdoor talks, surreptitious words (I even know some people who have done such things, ahem, ahem), but none like this. At half time. Of the championship game. By Club America, giant of Mexico, at home in Azteca.

Putting my immediate indignation aside (well, putting our glee at winning the title aside first), I thought we'll milk this for all we're worth and penned a snotty letter of complaint to all and sundry, not forgetting the wise man of Club America (and later the number 2 man at FIFA) Guillermo Canedo. He probably knew nothing about it and was, in fact, a very nice man but I was not letting that get in the way. So, we got $15,000 and all expenses paid for a game against Club America in Azteca, site of the World Cup final of 1970, and later 1986, and another game for cash against Vera Cruz.

About a year later, John Kerr was on the phone to Gordon Bradley begging to be bought back, which we did, much to the dismay of later leagues as John became the union firebrand and, in my mind, a true enemy of the progress of the game. I don't know if I ever told Gordon that John wasn't back long before he came in to see me and say that things were going badly with the team and Gordon didn't know what he was doing.

Club America had actually sent their man to see one of our other midfielders, the Pole Dieter Zajdel, the Man We Thought We'd Killed. It happened this way. Dieter was completely bald, though he was just over 32, the age when the Polish authorities allowed players to leave to try to earn some western currency before they got too old. So, Dieter turned up, bald, for a tryout and did not do too brilliantly; not enough, at any rate, to overcome the impression of age. So, thanks but no thanks, he was told. Next week, another Polish midfielder turned up, this one with a thick, thick mop of reddish-brown hair, and looked quite good until Charlie McCully went into a thundering tackle and sent this object flying off the other guy's shoulders and across the field. "I was sure it was his head," said a horrified Gordon Bradley. It wasn't. It was a wig. Underneath was bald-as-a-coot Dieter and we signed him and he won a deserved championship ring with us.

Which reminds me of Jerry Sularz, our goalkeeper, another one then at the age when the Communist government of his Polish homeland would let him out to see what scraps he could find in the West. Nearly 30 years later at a Cosmos reunion, Jerry, now plumper, grayer and much, much happier-looking than his old gloomy self, introduces his sons. It is noisy in the stadium so I didn't catch every word, but I know that one of them was at Harvard and the other was a doctor, I think. What is that saying about the American Dream?

They were casual, friendly times then and Werner Roth recalls: What I remember is being in the locker room for several games before finding out who these guys were who were rushing around handing out towels and things to the players. Then someone told me they were the owners, Steve Ross, Jay Emmett and Alan Cohen.

Yes, they were casual, friendly days and especially so when we won the NASL Championship. There was champagne, New York State champagne, in the locker room, I was lifted fully clothed, cigar alight, into the showers and came out sopping wet with cigar still going strong and we had an all round good time. Then. Five or ten minutes earlier it wasn't so casual and friendly and it happened this way.

It was, as I said, the NASL Championship game . . . a League affair, not a Cosmos-run game. All morning it poured down with rain. If the field had been grass instead of artificial turf, there would have been a swamp instead of a soccer field. As kick off time approached, the rain eased and a few brave souls started to emerge from their cars and a few more cars started to appear heading our way. It looked as if it would be one of those days most appropriate to our captain Barry Mahy's question: "Wouldn't it be quicker to introduce the fans to the players instead of the players to the fans." Along the lines of: And now, in row C, seat 16 is Joe Smith.

So, now what to do? The teams were there, the referee and linesman were there. Rain had definitely stopped. What had been a few hundred spectators had become somewhere in the low, very low, thousands and a decision had to be made whether to play or postpone. It was, as I noted, a League event; thus the Commissioner was the one to make that decision. Trouble was, he wasn't there; so I said "play."

When Phil did arrive, having been held up by flooded roads on his way to Long Island, he was not pleased; not at all and was even more prone to show his displeasure at the end of the game, as we were on the field celebrating. So, if you ever come across a picture of my wife grabbing me to celebrate on the pitch at Hofstra, do not be misled. She had observed the increasingly heated debate between Phil and myself and had run onto the field to stop me from punching him.

For the record, the line-up for that first Cosmos championship was: Richie Blackmore—Karol Kapcinski, Werner Roth, Barry Mahy, Dieter Zajdel, Siggy Stritzl, Josef Jelinek (sub Gordon Bradley), Randy Horton, Willy Mfum, Everald Cummings, Roby Young.

Five years later, the line-up for the next championship team had changed—and so, of course, had the cost. Only Werner Roth remained to collect a second ring in this team: Shep Messing—Paul Hunter, Werner Roth, Carlos Alberto, Nelsi Morais, Terry Garbett (sub Vito Dimitrijevic), Franz Beckenbauer, Steve Hunt, Tony Field, Giorgio Chinaglia (sub Jomo Sono), Pele.

HOW TO BECOME
A SOCCER MILLIONAIRE

OWNERSHIP IS A delicate, fragile thing and I do not jest. The right owner in the right place with the right attitude is a blessing. On the other hand, we could have given seminars on how to put your foot in it. For a start: Whatever did Philadelphia do to deserve us? We allowed some not-very-salubrious people to exercise their egos in a number of towns, but Philadelphia was given a double dose of not the way to do things.

It didn't start that way. Tom McClosky, a local construction company chief and wealthy enough to want an NFL franchise, bought an NASL one while he was waiting, named it the Atoms, hired Al Miller away from Hartwick College, did an absolutely first class job on and off the field and won the championship, with American players claiming starring roles. As their goalkeeper Bob Rigby said: "We had five American players on the field for most of the championship game but our success gave people the wrong idea about American players. People who wanted more Americans on the field pointed to our roster and said "See, they won the title with all those American players. Every team should do that." But a lot of American kids were not ready for the pros."

A year later two of them, Bobby Smith and Bob Rigby, were on their way to the Cosmos and a sea change must have occurred in Tom McCloskey's life because he was selected to own the Tampa Bay NFL franchise and rejected it, which is the only time that has happened, and then sold the Philadelphia Atoms to the United Clubs of Jalisco. If you're not a follower of Mexican football, let me explain. The State of Jalisco includes the city of Guadalajara. The city of Guadalajara contains four major league clubs—Universidad, Atlas, Jalisco and Guadalajara, nicknamed Chivas and the one that really matters; not just to Guadalajara but

to the ordinary people of Mexico, too. It is the people's team, the team of
the common man, it frowns on foreign players. It is the heart of Mexican
football in a nation where football is its bloodstream.

And these Mexican owners and a Mexican coach and whole host of
Mexican players moved into Philadelphia which, historic and a treasure
that it is, I have always considered somewhat dour, stolid, upright without
much merriment, no tinkling bells and gaiety in the streets, no large seg-
ment of the population speaking Spanish. Not even a Taco Bell back then.
I'm not talking about the more recent days of Mexifornia; of the ownership by Chivas, Guadalajara of Chivas USA, a team in Major League Soccer, playing in Los Angeles (well, there are more Mexicans there than in
Guadalajara).

I know it took me some considerable time to realize what a different
country I was in, despite the more-or-less common language, shared history, literature, outlook on life and several previous visits. Imagine the
impact on those poor souls from Mexico way back then. Imagine the harm
done to soccer in Philly. A year later, the franchise was sold to Montreal
and Philly lay bare. Three years later the cry may have been heard:
They're back, They're back. This time not with Mexicans but with rock
musicians and their agents, managers, lawyers, tour managers, record
executives, including two whom even I had heard of vaguely, Rick Wake-
man and Peter Frampton. (My musical interests and knowledge, while
varied, tend to lose their edge beyond the Massed Pipes and Drums of the
Highland Regiments, the Massed Bands of the Brigade of Guards, the US
Marine Corps Band, Louis Armstrong, Johnny Dodds, Sidney Bechet and
the whole massed group of ghosts of ancient New Orleans musicians, may
their names be once again known to more than some of us.)

With the British rock influence so strong in the ownership, a host of
British players were signed, that stadium with that rotten, rock-hard artificial surface was rented (I disliked it so much I can't remember its name,
or don't want to), great sums were spent on advertising and designer uniforms and such and the team stank. Peter Osgood, once the darling of
Chelsea—they called him the Wizard of Oz at Stamford Bridge—managed one goal in 22 games, a good part of the season was over before
some of the other big names arrived and Philadelphia fans still say it was
the worst managed club ever to set foot in the city, if not the league. There
would be some arguments about that last statement.

We came down for breakfast in the hotel after one early season game, and I was surprised to see a sizeable number of the Philadelphia players there, too, living, as I discovered, in the hotel, rather than out in the community. There were not sitting together; they were spread all over the dining room, each sitting with a different owner, each owner listening to "his" player. The show biz model of club ownership, perfected in New York. The big bosses undoubtedly have to listen with great care and sympathy in the acting and music business. In soccer, when owners listen to the cares and gripes of player, it is the kiss of death. So, Philadelphia once again took the path trodden once before and flogged the franchise to Montreal.

As has been said before. Owners should own, managers should manage, coaches should coach and players should play. Here are a few reasons why. Through my first six years of running the Cosmos, we, Gordon Bradley and I, chose the players, signed the players, put them on the field and told the owners who they were. Came 1977 and the stirrings at 75 Rockefeller Plaza that this thing was getting big, really big, and Jay Emmett asked me one day if I would please try to make Nesuhi Ertegun more involved, because he was starting feel left out and moan about it. So, I went up to Nesuhi's office and showed him a list of 11 players in whom we had some interest, to sign about three overall. As Nesuhi was a genuine soccer fan, as opposed to Steve Ross and his acolytes, I thought we would have a serious chat. Instead, Nesuhi looked at the list for a few moments and then said: We'll sign him, him, him, him and him. Two more than we needed but the worst part was—three of them were left backs.

I suppose it is understandable why owners get so totally carried away, obsessive, unable to accept anything except victory when they must have been that way in the first place to amass the money needed to be an owner . . . and get totally carried away, obsessive and absolutely unable to accept anything except victory. Plus the notion that their presence alone could move mountains. Steve Ross, Chairman of Warner Communications, was the epitome of all the above.

Very positive and decisive—look, I had said, there's this player called Pele and. . . Go get him, he said. OK, and now there's this other fellow, Franz . . . Right, he said, let's get him. So, who could ask for more than that? But more was what we got. The day before Pele's debut at Downing Stadium vs Dallas, we—the vast Cosmos staff of John O'Reilly, Gordon

Bradley, and sundry volunteers—were there trying to make some positive adjustments to a dump.

Rafael de la Sierra was spray painting the mud green so it would look like grass on CBS Sports, we were sweeping the stands (not something the City employees at the Stadium really liked to do; it, and general maintenance, got in the way of their jobs off-the-books elsewhere, I think) and Steve Ross arrived with a train of toadies in tow; looking where the great man looked, glaring ferociously where he glared, stopping where he stopped and nodding sagely when he stared in their direction. Finally, after the grand tour, Steve instructed that one ticket booth be moved so that it faced this way instead of that way. Great sighs of satisfaction all round; what a difference his being there had made. Hmmm.

It did on our first road game in 1976 to Miami. We were booked into the Marriott, not far from Miami airport, a perfectly acceptable team hotel, with proper meals booked and the team under control. One of them mentioned in Steve's hearing that he had heard a plane fly overhead and before you could say "spoiled brats," everyone was moved into the Fontainebleau on Miami Beach, with suites for all and instructions to eat whatever they liked and just sign for it. The first crack in the breakdown of discipline was upon us. It didn't help the atmosphere that Pele, of all people, missed a penalty before Dave Clements scored to give us the 1–0 win. Keith Eddy, our captain, told Pele that he, Keith, would be taking the penalties from then on and Pele sat in the john, door closed, crying.

I must admit, though, that Steve had amazing eyesight. Once we became big time, in 1976 at Yankee Stadium, he would peruse game videos obsessively and then I would be summoned on high to explain something he had spotted. Or more likely to be told something he had spotted, often the fact that a linesman had wrongly given, or not given, offside. And this from a fixed camera, staring at an angle of 45 degrees to the play where a linesman was making a split-second decision with a perfect view. And somewhere between 24 and 48 hours before. I am only thankful that later I watched games from the other side of Giants Stadium where he had a seat belt installed so that in his excitement he would not jump up and fall over the mezzanine. I know that's the kind of thing you might do to restrain a child—but the Chairman of a major public company?

There was also the poor fellow from Pittsburgh, back in '67, who told us at a League meeting: "We have a great team and we really don't want to run away with the league and make you guys look bad." They finished bottom and went away, bearing their apt name with them, the Phantoms. There were others, though, who were there at the start and there almost to the end. It is said the Chinese take the long view and thus Lamar Hunt should feel at home if he ever wants to emigrate from Texas. Lamar was as solid as a rock, counting pennies by such things as sharing a room with me on our expansion trips and years later counting out the millions to build the first major soccer-only stadium for his Columbus Crew in Major League Soccer. Lamar was one of a kind . . . he flew economy class and was alleged to have one jacket and one pair of pants "because that's all you could wear at one time."

At times, though, he seemed to have a relaxed, laconic attitude to money as Ted Howard remembers: We had a league conference call and in those days it wasn't so easy, people kept being dropped off or lost and we had to reconnect them and in one of the breaks Jim Ruben of the Minnesota Kicks said—hey Lamar, I've just been made head of General Mills apparel division. Lamar, as laconic as ever, said—that's great Jim. Yes, said Jim Ruben, we did 500 million dollars in business last year. What's that, Jim, said Lamar, about half a billion?

Bob Hermann, too, of St. Louis, George Strawbridge of the Tampa Bay Rowdies, the Robbies, Joe and Elizabeth, people heard from mostly when making sense, looking to the future and liking the game. Lee Stern of the Chicago Sting, too, though Lee was heard loud and often on every subject known to football-man, but a man who truly became in love with the game. To a greater extent than many others, they owned; they let their managers manage, their players play.

They did not, unfortunately, make up in the end for the others, the erratic, the Johnny-come-latelies and the carpetbaggers; entranced by the giant crowds and thinking all they needed to do was get a franchise, get a stadium and get some players and they'd be in the money. They also never heard, or never paid attention, to the mantra of the League: How do you become a soccer millionaire? Start with a billion.

10

IF YOU CAN'T SIGN
THE BEST . . .

THE WORLD CUP of 1974 in Frankfurt provided me with some childish delight. To get to Pele's suite for a half dozen different meetings, I had to pass the Media Center, then peopled by so many who were my contemporaries and with whom I spent time meeting and greeting as I strolled past on the way to or from a story they would all have loved to get. I always did enjoy getting an "exclusive."

On several occasions it looked as if Big Crocodile would not be coming. Big Crocodile was the code name we used in all correspondence, cables, wires, whatever (these were the days, believe or not, when we managed to conduct business around the world without faxes and e-mails) to identify Pele. On one occasion, therefore, I looked around and saw George Best. Indeed, George came out to New York, we had a really good talk and agreed I would be over to try to do a deal with Manchester United, which is what happened.

Knowing George's tendency to take life outside football rather more seriously than the game on occasion, we agreed on a 10,000 pounds, then about $12,000, down payment and another 10,000 every time he turned up fit to play. Les Olive, the United secretary, had the agreement typed; we signed and off I went to see George to finalize the deal, having seen him the night before in his club, Slack Alice, and told him all was going well. Trouble was, when Paddy Crerand, the United mid-fielder and George's occasional "minder," and I set off to find George, he could not be found. Not at home, not at any club, girl friend's house, bar, café, restaurant. Nowhere.

So I left a message—George, I shall be at Ringway Airport tomorrow morning, contracts in hand, until 11 a.m., when I fly back to New York.

See you then. Well, I didn't. Didn't see him again until the teams were lining up for an exhibition game between the Cosmos and Los Angeles
Aztecs in Tempe, Arizona. There was George in his Aztecs uniform, so I
walked up behind him and threw my arms around him and said "So, that's
where you got to, you little bugger." It's hard to be angry with George.
Mind you, it did give me a good line to use at one of the press conferences
when Pele finally signed. What about George Best now, someone asked.
Why sign George Best, I said, when you can sign THE Best.

There were times, mind you, when Besty was no more than a hairsbreadth
away from being level with Pele at the head of the line of the best-ever. If
his lifestyle, meaning booze and birds, had not foreshortened his career,
who knows how we would have viewed him in retrospect; certainly not as
the aged old man, a sunken-cheeked wreck, after a liver transplant late in
life and an early death. In better days, George was more like one of the
early Beatles and, in fact, acted like one on a flight from Rome to London
after we had flown in from Tirana, Albania, and a Northern Ireland World
Cup qualifier—which itself is worth a tale.

Albania was then impossible to visit, except for a soccer game, and
impossible to leave; there were more anti-aircraft guns pointing at the run-
way, in case someone should try to take off when not authorized, than
there were pointing to the skies for the invaders the Communist dictator
Enver Hoxha had told his people to expect. There were no private cars in
the country. The traffic cop, standing grandly on his box in the middle of
the vast Skanderbeg Square (Skanderbeg being the Albanian name for
Alexander the Great, whom they claim as their own) was mainly immo-
bile until, here it comes, a bicycle approaching, and, be careful, not one
but two horse-drawn carts, brought to a halt because here was an Army
truck, followed by a government car.

What traffic, what excitement; even if it did take more than 30 minutes for those few vehicles to enter the square. That is no exaggeration; I
stood and counted, dumbfounded that this was happening just an hour's
flight from Rome, its beauty and its nightmare traffic. The field on which
a World Cup qualifying game was to be played was mowed, of course. By
one man. With a push mower, the kind you would use for a postage stamp
of a lawn. That is all he had, poor soul, and I took a photograph to prove

it; that is until I made the mistake of pointing my camera at a government building, at which point my minder firmly insisted on taking my camera and removing the roll of film.

All countries behind the Iron Curtain provided "assistants" in those days, employees of the local security agency, of course, and in those dour, gray Eastern European countries of the time, the great excitement before and after filing stories was the frequent, and grimly frowned-upon, attempt to escape the hotel, through back doors, side doors, the kitchen, wherever, without being picked up by your minder. It rarely worked but when it did, and you approached the hotel entrance from the OUTSIDE, the look on the face of your guide and guardian was a treat to see. Mind you, when it did work, the poor sod probably got shot.

Well, back in this century and civilization, young, smiling, long-haired and good-looking, George was seated in front of a huge party of American tourists from Rome to London and when someone called out his name—George, of course—someone in the tourist party jumped to the conclusion that this George was George Harrison of the Beatles. His team-mates, when asked for confirmation, naturally inclined to do any-thing for a laugh, confirmed that he was, indeed, the Beatle and George spent the next hour merrily signing George Harrison's autograph and chat-ting away with delighted American tourists who, of course, could not tell one George's Scouse (Liverpool) accent from the other George's Ulster tones. If a better lifestyle had kept George going longer, and even better, it would have surely avoided the ludicrous situation of an internet poll in the 90s naming Eric Cantona as the greatest of all Manchester United players. Cantona should not be mentioned in the same breath as Best, nor with those who line up alongside him, and just behind Pele, people such as Eusebio, Beckenbauer, Maradona, Cruyff, Platini.

George in America was still a thrilling player, whether nutmegging two of Washington's Danish World Cup defenders inside three yards or taking the challenge from a tough-tackling team mate in San Jose who said he could take the ball off George inside a minute. George bet him $100 he could not, marked out a 12×12 area, and with the rest of the team counting down, touched and dodged his way past every tackle with complete aplomb until with a few seconds left, he kicked the ball at the challenger, tossed him the $100 bill and said "here you are, then, son"

In many ways, he was as much an icon of that age as David Beckham, then also of Manchester United, and also as much a part of a lifestyle different from his fellows as was George. I suspect that any more recent poll would have Beckham replacing Cantona as the greatest-ever at Old Trafford, which would be another travesty. And I say that even though I can still hear John Macadam, old when I was young and a writer of great prose, telling me that the players of his era, Alex James and Cliff Bastin and Hughie Gallacher, were far superior to the ones we were then watching. Maybe all of us in love with football have our own golden era, golden games and golden players. (But that still doesn't put Cantona or Beckham in the same locker room as George Best, so there.)

1974, though, was notable for something else, something worse. Indoor soccer is great for kids to learn skills in small spaces and have fun, great when the weather's bad and there's still the urge to kick the ball and have fun. It's also good even for the pros to practice on occasion and on occasion, though far fewer, to play a game and let the fans have some fun. But as a serious professional sport it is totally unacceptable to me, and plenty of others in the NASL, especially those whom it cost even more money and those club personnel struggling to find the time to organize and promote two different games, in two vastly different arenas, to two different segments of the populace and all within the same year. It was hopeless and a long running saga of indecision and interference with our primary activity. It started harmlessly enough in 1974, with a couple of games (see what I said above about occasional fun?) with an NASL All Star team against CSKA Moscow, the Red Army team, in Toronto and Philadelphia.

Next year we had regional tournaments, mostly with reserve players because so many of the better ones were back with their European clubs and the crowds were okay and it was a bit of fun for those with nothing better to do in that winter and the one which followed, 1976. The next year, the league's perpetual inconsistency showed up again with the decision to do nothing indoor, which brought all manner of people out of the woodwork. Jerry Saperstein, son of the founder of the Harlem Globetrotters, Abe Saperstein, dreamed up the modestly named Super Soccer League which never actually played a game. Down in Philadelphia, Ed Tepper, having seen the Red Army game in 1974, got together with a DC lawyer named Earl Foreman, and formed the Major Indoor Soccer League and the battle was joined; battle, in my view now as then, over territory not worth an exchange of rude words, never mind a fight to the death . . . which, in the end of course, it was; death for both MISL and NASL.

So MISL started in 1978. NASL started its indoor season in 1979, for those who wanted to play. Then NASL decided everyone had to play which meant an agonizing decision for some clubs. Did they put a different, lesser team on the field, thus risking disappointment and criticism from fans who'd grown to like the regular players who would normally go back home to play in the off season? Or did they now buy players outright, with the need for big transfer fees and full-time wages and permanent family relocations, instead of borrowing them inexpensively for the summer regular season? Not an easy decision to make, especially when the league changed its mind again and made the indoor season voluntary. By 1982, we were back to no season at all, though with Chicago, San Diego and Golden Bay (ex-San Jose) Earthquakes crossing over to play in MISL.

As bad as the inconsistency and player conflicts were, the actual operating of two different seasons was even worse. Instead of spending time promoting, hammering away at sponsors and season ticket and group sales for the next regular season, we were busy handling the day-to-day player, travel and game organization issues of an indoor season. In Toronto, when we reached Soccer Bowl in 1983, as we did again in 1984, we had a couple of weeks between Soccer Bowl and the start of a new indoor season. Try promoting that when you're traveling back and forward across the country in the play offs and busting a gut to get the best crowds and best coverage for your home playoff games. So the players could get overworked and over-tired. But it was the front office staffs who were the most affected, ridiculously so. It was hard enough selling one season. It was well-nigh impossible to sell two. MISL continued after we died and then joined us on the scrap heap. An unnecessary exercise and unwarranted competition over a game that could be fun on the odd occasion but had not the slightest scintilla of a chance of touching the tiniest corner of the canopy of soccer which covers the globe. So why bother?

But if 1974 brought us something bad, in the shape of indoor soccer, is also brought us something good; though we spent as much time hating it as we did respecting it, or them, as the case may be. The loathed and admired Tampa Bay Rowdies. Owned by George Strawbridge, of the Philadelphia Main Line, accent just a shade more American than English and impeccable manners, general-managed by Beau Rogers (T. Beauclerc

Rogers IV, that is), creators of that superb motto: Soccer is a Kick in the Grass and employers of the most vilified voice in American sports, their PA announcer Dick Crippen.

Tampa Stadium was crowded and noisy in those days, with crowds regularly in the 30,000 range, and more, and over all the roars, all the cheers, all the noise was Dick Crippen crying: What do you think of your Rowdies now? And the crowd would bellow back its approval. Not once; not twice, not a dozen times but every time those damned Rowdies did something remotely worthy of approval and those damned Rowdies often did something worthy of approval.

Iron Mike Connell at the back, Steve Wegerle up front on the right, the Clown Prince Rodney Marsh doing the simplest things the hardest way, just so everyone would enjoy themselves more . . . part of a team that gave Dick Crippen more than enough reasons to click the switch and cry again: What do you think of your Rowdies now? If that wasn't enough, Tampa's cheerleaders were called the Wowdies, so if the PA had to be silent on the team for a while, the Wowdies would shake their attributes about for a while and then would come the cry: What do you think of your Wowdies now? So, you would be back at the hotel after the game, beaten again as like as not, and cursing that voice and that name and all those people who had built such a following and such a feeling for that kick in the grass in Tampa.

I'm grateful to Marty Rotberg, one of the crew of Rowdies expert staff for insight into how it began. "The slogan," said Marty "along with the full marketing campaign for the Rowdies was developed by the ad agency McDonald and Little (Atlanta/Tampa), no longer in existence. When I joined the team at the end of the first season, they had already established a feel and marketing brand that was unlike anything that was done in sports at that time. George Strawbridge provided the money and the open mindedness, along with Beau Rogers, that was the impetus to develop a very unique sports franchise; all meant to persuade the football-mad Floridians that soccer was fun, entertaining and something they could embrace. The slogan became the center of everything the Rowdies did— TV, radio, newspapers and PR. The team became a phenom in Florida and many other franchises borrowed the lessons of the early Rowdies. The key ingredient was the commitment from management to allow smart people to be creative and spend money to communicate this new sport. Actually, I think Tom Little and a creative director from Australia came up with the original idea."

And actually I can still hear Dick Crippen now, asking: What do you think of your Rowdies? Well, they never were my Rowdies, Dick, but apart from wishing every last one of them to be stranded on a desert island and never found again (and that's the least punishment I wished on them at the time), I think they were great. Mike Lewis, once of the *Democrat and Chronicle* in Rochester and later on the New York *Daily News,* recalled the Rowdies fun didn't end when they did. "When Rodney Marsh later became a coach, he found the one way to get people to write about the kick off, the thing that no one ever writes about because there's nothing happening. He had all his players line up just as in (American) football and run down field after a long high kick."

Nobody else kicked off like Rodney but there was noise and color and promotions everywhere. Mind you, Dick Crippen's voice was not the only one to penetrate the consciousness. Another one was that of Jim Koerner, once of the Rochester Lancers (yes, them again) and later general manager of the St. Louis Stars, playing in cavernous Busch Stadium and coming in a bad third in the public mind to the Cardinals of baseball and football. So Jim decided to do something about it and one escapade is still in the mind of Jack Daley, then with the Toronto Metros and on a road trip to play the Stars.

"The fact that only five per cent of the stadium was occupied didn't faze Jim at all. He thought the big crowd was only just a game away and he would make people come through the power of radio," Jack explained. "He got time on a tiny 1000-watt station in the suburb of St. Charles. He produced and directed a pregame show, the actual game and the postgame show. In addition to selling all the advertising rights, Jim also hired himself as the on-air talent. Jim was a play-by-play marvel. He made the on-air game more exciting than it really was. Goalies were flying through the air to tip cannon shots over the bar. Game saving tackles were a dime a dozen and those deft passes through the middle and races up the wing left one hanging on every word. The commercials came fast and furious, too. Budweiser was frequently advertised throughout the game even though they did not sign on as a sponsor—Jim figured that after listening to one of his broadcasts, they'd eventually climb on board.

"But the highlight of his show was the "instant replay," a term he borrowed from the ever evolving world of television. We were watching the Stars and Metros one evening when he introduced me to his instant replay. He asked me to make a muffled crowd noise, like a low, building, roar when he gave me the cue. Sensing a break in the action, he announced to his audience that he was going to "rebroadcast" the tremendous run on goal by Casey Frankiewicz earlier in the half.

"Instead of pressing a button to reactivate the tape playback machine, Jim paused, took a deep breath and then went into a vivid description of Casey's run on goal, punctuated by me simulating, on cue, the roar of the crowd. When he stopped, I asked Jim: what on earth was that? My replay, of course, he replied. Great radio, eh? Jim, I asked, isn't this an odd thing to be doing? Don't you have the action on tape?

"Nope, too costly and time-consuming, was his reply. "Besides, I make it sound better the second time around and I didn't have any crowd noise then . . . now I do!"

What a wonderful world, what outrageous protagonists, what crazy stunts. Crazy George is the next to come to mind. Dressed in T shirt, ragged cut off jeans, banging a drum, he would descend from the rafters, a helicopter, appear from under the seats, on top of the roof, out of nowhere and anywhere, and begin beating that drum and rousing the crowd. But Crazy George was sane by comparison with many other promotions.

Noel Lemon had Captain Dynamite: "Captain Dynamite was a former World War II demolitions expert. He wore a silver suit and a crash helmet and had this papier mache coffin in the center circle and he would lie down in it, as the PA announcer counted down from ten, and then he'd set off the explosives packed in alongside him and you'd get this enormous explosion. Fragments flying everywhere and smoke so you couldn't see a thing and then you'd see his legs twitch and his arms flopping around and he would stand up and the crowd loved it.

"One day, Ian Greaves, the Bolton Wanderers manager, was being interviewed on TV at half-time when Captain Dynamite did his thing and they both jumped out of their skins when the explosion went off, then the cameras went to the field to see Captain Dynamite and when it switched back to them they were both laughing too much to speak. All Ian Greaves could say was that back in England they preferred to bomb (meaning fire) managers when they didn't like them. So Captain Dynamite staggered to the bench and the subs sat down when the teams came out and Bill Foulkes, our coach, came out last and sat on the other end—and jumped out of his skin when he looked down and saw smoke coming out of some-one down at the end of the bench. Anyway, he cost us $1000 for the performance, so we brought him back again later. The trouble was that by then a brand new artificial turf field had been laid and it was harder, so he misjudged the amount of explosives he needed and blew and bloody great hole in the new artificial turf. That was the end of that.

> "But the University of Tulsa people came to me one day and said what did I know about dozens of loaves of bread being dumped outside the stadium behind one goal? So we went to take a look and there they were . . . great piles of bread and I looked across the street, saw this baker and realized what had happened. We had a promotion with the bread distrib-utor—a coupon for a $3 discount on a reserved seat. So people were going in, buying a loaf of bread for 50 cents and saving 2.50 on a ticket. Proof that the promotion was working, I suppose. We had all kinds of mascots, one in this great rabbit outfit and one day he got carried away. There was a fight on the field and the next thing there was the rabbit out on the field trying to separate the players. That must have been a shock to them, this giant rabbit suddenly appearing but the referee was not pleased."

Elsewhere, there were Armadillo races, when no part of their anatomy seemed to move despite encouragement, to Halter Top races, when certain parts of the anatomy were plainly moving vigorously. Or as Dick Berg, originator of those and many other adventurous forms of entertainment, was heard to describe it: "78 boobs bobbing up and down the field."

Berg and fellow GM John Carbray invented the Bang Box and Box Penetrations, or in plain language, vividly painted penalty areas—the Bang Box—and a brand new statistic, the number of times a team got the ball into the Bang Box. It helped the often psychedelic flavor of so many soccer fields at the time, so often with American Football markings, and home team logos, painted immoveable, and soccer's plainer, leaner lines in yellow. Many a throw-in was taken from the wrong line, believe me.

Sometimes it felt as if you needed sunglasses to lessen the glare from so many colors and so many markings.

Gordon Bradley recalled: "I forget where they were, but there was this one stadium, Portland, I think, with a grassy bank at one end and this guy came charging down the bank and onto the field in a chariot and the bloody wheel came off. Then somewhere else, they had this helicopter land—after a long wait because we were underneath the flight path of a nearby airport—and out came this gorilla, holding the ball. Well, he didn't know which way to go, because there was chaos outside the helicopter, and the gorilla started coming towards the bench. You've never seen benches clear so fast. We must have been 35, 40 minutes late kicking off by the time the whole thing was sorted out." But we did have a new slogan: Soccer—The Sport of the Eighties.

We also had as much bizarre behavior behind the scenes as we did in public. Noel Lemon, again, on a play-off game at Giants Stadium against the Cosmos. "It was a wet rainy night, everyone slipping and sliding and in the first minute someone hit a cross from the right and the ball went skipping over the surface past about eight players and there was Chinaglia at the far post to knock it in. One down and we went on to lose 8–1 and Chinaglia got seven of them. Well I went into the locker room and had a nice, pleasant conversation with the team, steam was coming out of my head, and then went up into the Stadium Club for a drink. I didn't realize it but I was standing in front of the service bar and the bartender said—move, you're in the way—and I told him what to do with himself and he lifted the bar flap and came out to see me. Well, what I didn't realize is that the floor behind the bar was sunken, about two feet down, so when the guy came out he must have been about 6-feet 9 and he said—do you have a problem?—and I said damn right I do, we just lost 8–1 and he said—well, I'm sorry sir—and went back behind the bar.

"I had told the team, nobody speaks to the press about this, nobody, except the coach. If you do, it'll cost you. So next day one of the Tulsa papers quoted an unidentified player as saying they had been told by me not to talk to the press. Well, a couple of months later they came looking for their play-off bonus money and I said—what bonus? I told you it would cost you if you talked to the press, I've paid all your play-off bonuses to charity, the Special Olympics."

The conundrum of Bob Bell, owner of the San Diego Sockers, was more expensive. "I have these two Mexican players on loan and I can buy either of them, can't afford both, which one should I take?" He signed a good midfielder in Leonardo Cuellar. He let the other one go, to become the greatest goalscorer in the history of Mexico and Real Madrid, Hugo Sanchez by name.

Noel Lemon, yes, again, showed how internal promotion can help sometimes, too. "We were having this terrible road trip. We had a standing ovation in San Jose, a great game, we were two down, came back to 2–2, went down 3–2 with about a minute to go, came back and made it 3–3 with seconds left and then lost 4–3 in overtime. In Vancouver we went to the penalty shoot out and Johnny Giles of the Whitecaps, standing next to me, said they couldn't score a penalty to save their lives in practice. So we scored five . . . and they scored six.

"On to Edmonton and I said to the bus driver—is there a Skid Row area in town, so take us there. And we pulled up outside this terrible hotel, people on the streets drinking out of brown bags, litter everywhere, it was terrible. So as the bus pulled up, I said OK, let's go, and the players started muttering 'What's this?' and young Joe Morrone said 'My mother wouldn't let me go in there', but I got them out and we walked into the lobby—one bulb hanging from the ceiling, this guy behind the counter, half-asleep, and as the players looked around in horror, I asked the desk clerk: OK, you have the Tulsa Roughnecks' rooming list?

And he looked at me in complete ignorance . . . and then I couldn't hold it in any longer. I just burst out laughing and they started calling me an idiot and god knows what else, and we got back on the bus and went to our proper first class hotel. We beat the crap out of Edmonton the next day."

The last words in this chapter of loonies belongs, though, to Shep Messing (he of the nude photo in Playgirl, pet cobra in the bathtub, Harvard, the only man who ever sued me, well, so far anyway) and Bobby Smith, the hard man from Trenton. We are playing in Los Angeles. Shep is in goal, Smithy at right back. They have, so it turns out, been out on the town the night before, the morning before, and are under real pressure from the start. A corner for LA; cleared. Another corner and then another corner, and yet another, all within the first two minutes. As Smithy takes up position by the near post, resting on it as much as guarding it, he calls to Shep: How much longer to go?

That, by the way, is the same tough young man who, years later at a Cosmos reunion at Giants Stadium and addressing a new crop of young MetroStars, told them: "That wasn't a locker room in there. That was heaven. That's still my locker room in there even if my name's not on it, next to Carlos Alberto and he's saying I had a good game and I can't believe Carlos Alberto is saying that about me. That's heaven. And when the time comes for you to leave, too, you'll know what I mean." Sooner or later, this game gets to you.

THE DAY PELE SPLIT HIS PANTS

NOW WE WERE into the fifth year, the fifth year of the Cosmos, the fifth year of the persuasion of Pele and more remarkable than the fact that the chase was still continuing was the fact that no one knew about it, except for a very tight inner circle. Pele, of course, and his brother Zoca and Mazzei; the tiny Cosmos staff now expanded to four with the addition of Cynthia Kingdon, yes four . . . Gordon Bradley, John O'Reilly, Cynthia and me, not exactly the largest staff in the known professional sports world.

So that makes seven people at least partly in the know. Then across at Warner, where busy men ran major businesses, there was some current knowledge of the progress I was making, or lack of it, by Steve Ross and Jay Emmett and Nesuhi Ertegun and help from Rafael de la Sierra but as I never discussed it with anyone else, I have no idea who or if anyone else had a clue about it. Whenever I met with the Pele, we met secretively. Whenever we communicated, we did so by never mentioning Pele's name. Ever. He was Big Crocodile, that was Julio Mazzei's chosen cover name for Pele, and never anything else. Then something leaked from Brazil and there, for the first time, was the media attention.

PELE STORY PUBLICITY HOAX, ran the headline, with two immortal lines to follow after general criticism of anything and everything: "The latest was the Pele hoax. It was nothing short of that, an unfortunate ploy for a line or two in the papers just when the season began, hoping to hype fan interest and sell some tickets, Pele wasn't going to the United States to play any more than Moshe Dayan would join the Egyptian Air Force."

That, in a Rochester, New York newspaper by a reporter whose blushes I shall spare, is the first and one of the few stories I remember from those impossible days. The poor sap, having no idea of the excruciating care we had taken over the years of effort, went on for 19 paragraphs lambasting us for our duplicity and falsehoods. I know its 19 paragraphs, I just counted them. That was one clipping I could never part with. But there wasn't much else at the time, with mostly disdain being shown overall for the story added to the Rochester disbelief and with a general shrugging of the shoulders at such palpable nonsense and so the chase continued and was nearing its end, one way or the other.

By early in the year I had, for many reasons, decided this was the last charge. It had taken too long, taken too much out of me, taken me away too much from that tiny staff, leaving them with more work than was right and proper. It was now time and the place was Belgium. The GB Motor Hotel, on the fringes of Brussels' airport, figures in no travel brochure and attracts no group of tourists but history was made there on "The Day Pele Split His Pants." It was actually "The Day He Agreed To Play for the Cosmos" but its that other bit of Monty Python absurdity that sticks in the mind just as much and this is how it happened.

It was March 27, 1975; it says so on the piece of Hotel notepaper, just below his signature and a few handwritten lines headed Pele's Last Proposition. It was, in fact, his first—the first time he said he would sign for the Cosmos after four years and one month of tracking him through the world, pestering him to death and wearing him down. As far as I was concerned, this was the last gasp; the last time I would sit with him and Julio Mazzei and find every fragment of persuasion to get him to play. Along the way, in Jamaica, in Toronto, in Frankfurt, in Sao Paulo and Santos and Guaruja, in—well, I've forgotten all the places—he moved a little . . .

I'll do some clinics for you, he said somewhere along the way. Thanks, but not enough. I'll play a few exhibition games for you. Hmmm, nice but not what we need. Well, now I can't do anything for you. Well, let's not say goodbye, let's meet again, maybe, just maybe we'll find common ground somewhere. And so, we met in Brussels because he was playing in the testimonial game for Paul Van Himst, the captain of Belgium and later national coach of Belgium in the 1994 World Cup in the USA. We met there in the Belgian capital and so did a couple of dozen of the world's great stars to play in the game on a wet and chilly night. So we will meet, I thought, at length and in private and I will use my last best lines and either succeed or fall on my sword. So I thought because I wasn't the only one, surprise, surprise, who wanted time with Pele.

I flew in from New York, he flew in from Sao Paulo and before we had time to exchange more than pleasantries, it was off to a glittering reception hosted by the Minister of something or other. No time to talk, the first evening gone but tomorrow for sure. No, not tomorrow because then it was off to lunch at Van Himst's home and then Pele had to rest for the game that night and then there was the game . . . and then there was one morning left, four years and one month of trying and just one morning left. One morning before he had to catch a lunch time plane to Casablanca on the start of a promotional tour around the Mediterranean which would end in Rome in two weeks time. One morning, one quiet morning with Pele and Mazzei and me in Pele's room and my final speech in mind.

So we talked. We sat and talked. We stood and talked as Pele quietly packed. And then it began. Midway through a sentence and a rap on the door. Bloody hell, I thought, go away. Instead in came Eusebio to say goodbye . . . hugs, kisses, goodbye. Ok, start again, and in came Rivelino, and then came Alan Simonsen and then came . . . well, they all came. One by one, the stars of the world to say goodbye to the biggest of them all, innocently ruining my every thought, my every hope, my last remaining moments of hoping for success. The worst was the arrival of Jose Altafini, the last man to play in a World Cup for two different countries—Brazil and Italy—before FIFA changed the rules. A great goalscorer was Altafini for both his countries and AC Milan, an ebullient character, a player I would have signed on the spot . . . except not on this day and not on this spot, which was what Jose proposed the minute he saw me. I did tell you Brazilians aren't shy about such things, didn't I?

Aha!, he said, or something like that, trying to sign Pele, eh? Well, sign me as well. Not now, Jose, please not now. But he was persistent and quite oblivious to the fact that there were other vital things afoot and that is what I was concentrating on. So I made him an offer, an insulting offer, to make him go away and he did . . . and gave me many dark looks in later years despite my trying to explain and apologize. But, go away he did, and peace reigned and Pele packed and, knowing Juventus and Real Madrid were still interested in signing him, I said—sign for them and all you can win is a championship, sign for me and you can win a country. It was a pretty good line then and its pretty good even today but before I had chance to see if it worked, Pele finished dressing, pulled on his pants, tight, tight, pants . . . and split them down the seam. Oh bugger it, I thought as Pele took off his trousers, wrapped a towel around his waist and Julio rang for the chambermaid to come with a needle and thread.

So, in she came. A respectable, middle-aged lady who took one look at Pele and burst into tears. What on earth now, I thought, and in a muddle of English, French and lord knows what else, she told us. Her husband had been a massive fan of Pele. He had never seen him play. He had bought an expensive ticket for the game last night. He had died of a heart attack two weeks ago. His son had used the ticket but, for sentiments sake, could she have a photograph taken with Pele? So, amid tears and time passing and my frustration of four years and a month going to naught, she went to get a camera and mend Pele's pants and finally we sat and talked and he said yes, he would play.

For two years. For $2 million plus plus plus, amounting to about $3 million. Put that on paper and sign it, I said, and he did. Now, I said, that's not good enough, I need three years because in the third year Giants Stadium will be built and that is where I want the Cosmos to play and that's where you have to be. I don't think that bit really registered because now the poor lady was back, camera in one hand, pants in the other, and Pele dressed, the photos were taken and we were late for the plane to Casablanca. Not that I need to have worried and not that Pele ever worries about such things because when he arrived at the airport, all was chaos. People came charging in all directions once someone recognized him; immigration officers, passport control, passengers, ground staff, even, finally, the pilots of his aircraft came running out to greet him.

And off he went. And back to the hotel went I to have lunch and two, yes two, of the most expensive bottles of wine on the menu. We were almost there. As Sir Winston Churchill had said about something far more important after the Battle of El Alamein, it was not the end, it was not the beginning of the end, but it was the end of the beginning, albeit a beginning of four years and one month.

Two weeks later we met in Rome and I made him a formal offer, over dinner at the Hotel Excelsior on the Via Veneto. "Toye, " he said "my English is not good." It's fine, Pele, I replied encouragingly and somewhat mystified. "No, he said" in Brussels I say $3 million for two years and you offer me less money for three years. My English is not good." But we kept talking, between the usual interruptions. Would he sign the chef's hat? Of course. Would he sign a ball for one of the young kitchen workers if the lad rushed home to get it? Certainly. Would he take the guitar of the strolling musicians and play to the packed and elegant restaurant? Yes, he would and did because he is an accomplished musician. Would he, said a gentleman in frock coat and blazing decorations, come with him into a huge diplomatic reception in a private room and honor them all by taking a glass of champagne? Yes, he and we, duly followed and the crowd of the most dignified diplomats and the society of Rome rose in adulation.

But now it was serious. The lawyers and accountants were hovering, the numbers were being massaged and Pele went for the necessary medical the next day. As he lay on the table, the doctor said that the beautiful Romy Schneider had been there a little while before, which certainly piqued Pele's interest. He passed the physical, of course, and all we had to go through now was another two months of fine tuning and final persuasion, in New York and Santos and Sao Paulo and Guaruja and Guaruja and Sao Paulo and Santos and enough miles on Varig and Pan Am to go to the Moon and back, so it seemed.

The strength of a major corporation now played its part, with Jay Emmett on hand to negotiate the points of the non-Cosmos, nonplaying agreements. There was a public relations deal with Warner Communications itself. A music deal with one of Warner's stable of music companies, Atlantic or Warner. A marketing rights deal with Licensing Corporation of America, so that it was not just Pele the player we were buying, it was Pele the brand for resale to the world's major companies. Even then with Pele prevaricating still and telling us the Brazilian government and populace were against this move, we enlisted the aid of Congressmen and kids, who sent hundreds of letter, including one from my 9-year-old son Robert telling Pele he could stay at our place if he came, and then enlisted Henry Kissinger to send through a message that this was a great opportunity for Brazil to help develop the game and make millions of Americans ever grateful to them for letting this national treasure depart.

It was close, it was narrowing, it was falling apart, thousands of legal documents in English and Portuguese, lawyers almost coming to blows one night in Sao Paulo, a wire service story that Pele had spurned a $7 million dollar offer. And then Warner sent a private jet to fly Pele and his wife Rose and Mazzei and Zoca from Sao Paul to Hamilton, Bermuda, we flew out from New York, Jay Emmett and Rafael and myself, to sign the contracts in the Hamilton Princess Hotel and life was never the same again. There was a last minute snag. I told Pele that the USSFA charged $15 to register a player and that the rules were that the player had to pay it, though not true, of course. Pele looked at me in absolute astonishment, then laughed and took a $10 bill and a $5 bill from his pocket, signed them and handed them over; knowing, of course, that those were two precious bills I would never hand over and we would have to pay the $15 in any case. Now two corporate jets flew us all back to New York, ready for a press conference and a hastily arranged exhibition game against the Dallas Tornado, because as luck would have it we had no league game that week, an even hastier deal with CBS for the telecast, no time to eat, no time to sleep, no longer were we "who?," we were the Cosmos and our number 10 was Pele.

The 21 Club is one of the haute monde nosh and booze places in New York City, if I may use that term to describe its rather snooty, $29 hamburger and "you're lucky we let you in" attitude. Which is why I choose the 21 Club and its Hunt Room for the Pele press conference. It was a symbolic move. Soccer was always 14th Street and no further uptown than the McAlpin Hotel on 34th Street, where the longtime promoter Enzo Magnozzi held court. The 21 Club is 52nd Street, just off Fifth Avenue. We, and soccer, had arrived. From the behavior of the media, we should have moved a dozen blocks north to Central Park Zoo. We'd had crowds not much bigger than the photo corps, stretched in rows, from wall to wall, shoving, pushing, elbowing, kneeling, falling over, cursing and flashing. I wasn't expecting it; I had never seen media, not even photographers for heaven's sake and you know how ill-mannered they are, behave so badly. It was also the first time Pedro Garay, a Cuban exile, with misty tales of a former CIA existence trailing behind him, came into action.

Rafael de la Sierra, a Cuban exile himself, had hired Pedro as Pele's bodyguard, a job he did with great sincerity but in such a manner as to bring mirth to others so many times. I was trying to control the mob too much to notice exactly when and where Pedro suddenly disappeared but Werner Roth, captain and center half of the USA and the Cosmos and later to feature as that nasty captain of the German team in the John Huston movie "Victory," along with Pele and many other stars, had a better view. Werner was at the back of the room with a half dozen of the players and relayed his tale of the day this way: "You were on the dais, which was separated from the media by a row or two of tables, covered by white tablecloths. Two photographers were in a fist fight and you were saying: Gentlemen, Gentlemen of the Press, and nobody was taking any notice of you, so Pedro decided to stop the fight and stepped forward on to the tables. The trouble was the tables were not connected, it looked as if they were, but there were gaps covered by these tight, white tablecloths. And Pedro stepped on to one of the gaps, disappeared down under the tables and was never seen for the rest of the afternoon."

We had to get used to such mayhem. When you are with Pele, all norms of civilized behavior tend to come to an end. But before the mayhem continues, a moment of silence here for Angelo Anastasio. Who? Well, we had a league regulation allowing a maximum of 18 players on the roster at any one time. We had 18 players. We signed Pele. One had to go. It was Angelo, a hard working and not bad right back from Adelphi Unversity, whose claim to fame is the boast: I was cut from the roster to make way for Pele.

For many of the players who remained, it was a difficult time because many of them did not want to play with him. What they wanted to do was watch him play, just delight in watching him play and some admitted they found themselves doing that, even when they were on the field with him. The adoration of fellow professionals may be best shown by the tiny episode involving Gil Mardarescu, our midfielder from Roumania. He approached Pele, crossed himself and said: "I dreamed of some day of just shaking your hand. But to play with you, this is a miracle." And, when I think back on it, that's just what it all was. Now, we had the publicity, the crowds and forewarning of the attention that was to come from the rich and famous so give Robert Redford some credit. We had half of Hollywood strolling round the place before the end but he came to see us play at Randalls Island. It isn't worth a medal but is certainly worth a mention.

We also had attention from the famous but not-yet-so-rich. Out of the blue, the President of FIFA, the Brazilian Dr Joao Havelange called one day to ask for a meeting "about commercial matters." Remember, we had spent $2.8 million on acquiring Pele . . . not Pele as a soccer player alone, but Pele the man, Pele the name, Pele the image . . . and already Pepsi Cola, Honda and Pony had paid back substantial sums to buy pieces of the Pele "brand." Havelange wanted to see if we could do the same for FIFA which, before him was an organization devoted to football and from his election onwards was an organization devoted to making money out of football.

One of Warner's divisions, Licensing Corporation of America, had been the obvious vehicle to exploit Pele and thus Warner and LCA executives and I met with President Havelange, with me thinking what an incredible coup this was going to be. Well, it wasn't. Next day the word came down to me that the brains of the outfit could not see any business there and I had to carry that strange news to Havelange who went off to make billions for FIFA with other enterprises. It only came to me later, when the rot had set in, that here was a major corporation whose top brass could see a player offside from a 45-degree angle, 24 hours after a game, as I explained, but couldn't see the value of doing business with FIFA.

But that was in passing. Now the world—and match fees—awaited us and off we went on our first Pele tour, first stop Sweden where he had first been seen by the world on TV, as a 17-year-old winning the World Cup in 1958 and captivating us all. We landed in Copenhagen and on the car ferry to Malmo had a seagoing press conference in the bow of the ship along the way. But after a day or so in Malmo we saw the first signs that the awe of having Pele among us was wearing off a little as we waited in the team bus, somewhere around the 50th team bus we had taken since his arrival and for the 50th time he was late and the irritations were slowly eating away at the awe. I went to the glass front of the hotel to see if there was any sign of him and there was . . . way back at the elevators, there he was surrounded by a crowd, slowly progressing, signing autographs, smiling. And I realized, of course, that Pele never walks anywhere alone in public and what takes the rest of us a few moments takes him an age.

So from then on, I posted two different schedules for the team. One at the right time for the mortals and one 30 minutes earlier for Pele. Awe is not too strong a word to use in our relationship with Pele, for the players who were partly embarrassed to play with him and partly wishing they could just sit in the stands and watch him play and for me, too. My early PR biographies stated, quite truthfully, that my three heroes were Winston Churchill, Louis Armstrong and Pele. Well, I had seen Churchill once in the distance, had heard Armstrong play once in London but here was the third one of that heroic trio, actually working for me. It was not always easy to know how to separate the icon from the player.

That whole tour was a blur even at the time but some things and some people and some places stand out even now. Prime Minister Olle Palme of Sweden came to see us: "When I tell my family I am meeting kings and queens, presidents and prime ministers, they shrug their shoulders. When I told them I was coming here to meet Pele, they all wanted to come." Then Oslo and the only time I swore in front of royalty. Sitting on the right of King Olav, uptight as I always was during games and cautioned that one never speaks to royalty until royalty speaks to you, I still could not hold it in when one of our defenders made an absolutely atrocious mistake. "You stupid bugger," I blurted out. "He is, isn't he," said the King.

Kingston, Jamaica. We had this enormously courteous private meeting with Jamaican Prime Minister Michael Manley and then faced a different reception at the stadium; a stadium packed to about 150 per cent capacity, so much so that spectators were six deep all around the touchlines, and there was no way I could get through the crowd to go up to the VIP seats. So, I sat on the bench and within moments, the crowd was thick beside us, behind us and in front of us and they were not all friendly, not even to Pele, calling him vile names, telling him he had sold his soul to the white man and generally making things unpleasant.

Security man Pedro Garay was on the bench, too, and when Pele was injured, sat beside his charge. Behind us, and slowly inching his way on his buttocks towards Pele, was this gnarled old Jamaican and when he got close, he reached up and touched Pele, that's all, a touch. Pedro snarled at him to stop. He didn't. He touched Pele again and Pedro jumped up and began to get truly vociferous. Well, here we were, one black guy, Pele, and a small group of white men, sitting in a sea of Jamaicans many of whom were showing signs of increasing hostility and Pedro wanted to thump this one harmless old man. So I yelled at Pedro and we jumped at him and forced him to sit down and shut up and hoped we would survive. It did get nastier. Someone ran on the field, the Red Stripes (Jamaica's name for their cops as well as their beer) ran on with huge sticks and began to beat him, Pele ran on and stooped between their sticks and the man being beaten, but when the game ended, we had everything under the sun thrown at us on the way to the locker rooms and stayed in there, somewhat concerned, for over an hour as people tried to smash their way in with fists, sticks and lord knows what.

We were very, very late that night and very early next morning en route to the airport and a nice lady turned up asking if Pele would record a message on camera telling Jamaican youth to stay off drugs and be good kids, that sort of thing. Well, Pele was so tired he looked gray rather than black but he agreed and the camera was switched on and . . . out came this bright and beaming face, the smile, the voice and the perfectly phrased message to all the kids and parents watching. Quite a switch, quite a pro.

Rome. We closed down Rome's Fiumicino Airport. All the baggage handlers there used to wear, maybe still do, these bright orange bibs.

When our plane pulled up on the tarmac, a long way from the terminal, to wait for the bus, I looked out the window and saw hundreds, hundreds, of men in orange vests swarming towards our plane, to cluster in a great congregation around the bottom of the stairs to await Pele's descent. I looked around everywhere . . . there was not a single movement anywhere on the ground at Fiumicino, none, no plane being loaded or unloaded, no fuel being added, no little trucks buzzing around, nothing except the jostling throng awaiting Pele.

Port au Prince, Haiti.   We're in the bus, again, a battered old school bus, which was the best they could do for us, and waiting again for Pele, while the driver, with hat pulled over head, snoozes at the wheel. Slowly the heat builds in the bus for which no air conditioning was ever intended and so does the heat in the comments on Pele tardiness, late even for him. About the time the remarks are going to get really bad, the bus driver starts to shake with laughter, takes of his hat and turns with a big smile on his face. It's Pele. Rome, Tokyo, Port au Prince, Kingston, Gothenberg, Osaka, Oslo, Malmo, Central Park, New York. It makes no difference. If Pele's there, so is the crowd.

Central Park, you say? What's that about Central Park? Well, it is now 1994 and Pele has been retired for 17 years and we are in a very quiet, shady area of New York's Central Park, just Pele and Mazzei and I and two or three people from ABC's *Good Morning America* because Pele and I are about to be interviewed by Andrew Shue about the upcoming World Cup. We are a small, quiet group, way out of sight, under trees at the south end of the Sheep Meadow.

One teenager passes by, looks, turns away, swivels his head back for another look and then takes off at a run across the park. Julio Mazzei says to me: Oh my, there'll be a crowd here in a minute. And I say, no Julio, that's silly and he says: want to bet? And I say yes and I lose. There are a couple of minutes before I lose when all remains tranquil and then they come streaming across the park, over the lawn, out of the trees, running in from the street. There are hundreds of them—seventeen years after he last kicked a ball, this dark-skinned man sitting in deep, dark shade under the trees but still recognized and once recognized never alone in any country on earth. Don't even think of comparing the global recognition and adoration of Michael Jordan or Tiger Woods or even Mohammed Ali.

We came back from our first Pele tour in time to "announce" another signing. Warner Communications owned a place out in New Jersey at the time called Jungle Habitat so some bright spark came up with the idea one day of "signing" one of their animals and having a press conference to announce it. It was quite harmless fun and turned hilarious when Harold the Chimp showed us what he thought of the whole thing. He urinated copiously on all the press releases. I could have done with him a few other times, too. So many targets and only one Harold.

We came back, too, with memories of those marvelous stadiums in which we had played, even in poor, pitiable Port au Prince was there a stadium for soccer, Stade Silvio Cator, which made our home in New York seem a disgrace. Which, of course, it was. Wrote one of the growing Cosmos press corps: Watching Pele play at Randalls Island is like seeing Baryshnikov dance in a Times Square honky tonk joint. I would claim that line as my own if I could. But I have much more to say about Downing Stadium than that.

ALL WE WANT IS SOME LAND, SOMEWHERE

DOWNING STADIUM ON Randalls Island, in the middle of the East River, the center of New York City: Built as a Works Projects Administration (WPA) project in the days of the Depression, one of the most important programs in President Roosevelt's New Deal, giving work to 8 million people in those terrible times. Then left to rot by the City of New York. There was often no water in the locker rooms, except that which overflowed from the toilets on the floor above; very little grass, with the dirt spray-painted green for Pele's debut so it would not look so bad on CBS (though it did look bad on Pele; he found his feet covered in green fungus, or so he thought, and worried he had attracted a dangerous skin disease. Try explaining the truth to a man who had played on the greatest fields in the world). No regular security so that the Press Box was broken into regularly, no matter how many locks or reinforced doors and barricades we put in place; a City-employed, union work force which, in the main, considered manual labor (i.e. moving about) not included in their maintenance and cleaning job descriptions.

This led to the sight of the coach, Gordon Bradley, John O'Reilly, our PR man, and others grabbing brooms and sweeping the stands themselves before games after some HS track meet or whatever, so that our fans wouldn't be stepping through garbage to get to their seats and sitting on trash when they got there. It was also, on game days, frequently staffed by crooks, er, well, union members who didn't actually bother to negotiate better deals for themselves, they just made their own arrangements. I found out about this when we played Napoli and someone came rushing up to me to say tickets were being scalped in the parking areas.

This was, of course, a novel experience for us and I was quite elated until he told me they were being scalped for half price. So, not success after all but something wrong and it was this: The ticket takers were palming whole tickets, knowing the rabid Napoli fans were in too much of a rush to worry about such niceties like getting a ticket stub so they could see where they were supposed to sit, and then passing them in bulk to a confederate standing to the rear. This man then went up the stairs to the second level where huge open porticos allowed him to throw down the tickets, wrapped in a handkerchief or plastic bag, to a third man who walked out into the parking lot and sold them. This was the first example I came across in New York City of recycling. It looked as if we had about 14,000 in the place that day; we took in enough money for about 7,000— and then hired our own security staff, one behind each ticket taker.

This was the place where Pele made his debut for the Cosmos, on a day when the place was so packed if you blinked an eyelid you hit someone; the place where we found out that while it wasn't easy to get there from here, wherever here might be, it was damned impossible to get from there back to here in anything less than an age. Let me explain. For those who don't know New York, Downing Stadium was on Randalls Island, in the shadow of the gigantic Triborough Bridge which, as the name suggests, connects, with massive road ways and tolls, the three New York City boroughs of Queens, The Bronx and Manhattan and over which pours an endless stream of traffic from Long Island, Connecticut, Westchester and tractor trailers from all points on the map.

Down from that maelstrom of machines slips one roadway, down to Downing Stadium, down which your crowd must go and up which it must go in return on the way home. Now, it isn't so much of a problem when your crowd numbers under 10,000, say, which is a limit we managed to achieve quite handily, thank you, until Pele arrived. It isn't even an unmanageable problem with a big crowd on the way in. After all, people arrive at games in their own time, flowing in their time, early, late, whenever. But when a game ends, everyone leaves at the same time. And is confronted by a wall of traffic, all heading for that one roadway to the traffic of Triborough Bridge.

I was not conscious of the enormity of the problem on that first Pele day. It was a Sunday afternoon, there was plenty of time and everyone was flushed with the excitement of it all. But the following Wednesday we played again, Pele's league debut, and we had about 17,000 on hand and long did they stay there. After the usual locker room conversations and exhortations, after the media chat, I recall walking out and seeing this parking lot of a roadway, thousands still standing by their cars, busloads of people still milling around because they and their bus were not going anywhere; so I went back inside again and it is just as well I did. It was about 11 pm when the phone calls started—that's two hours after the game ended—from people asking if we knew why so-and-so hadn't got home yet. Quite a number, I recall well, were from anxious parents out on Long Island whose children were on those buses of youth soccer groups brought in to see the man himself, in the flesh. Did we know if anything had happened, had there been an accident? Well, no, we said, their off-spring were probably still out in the parking lot and the only accident was that when the stadium was built, with that one access road, people didn't have cars in such numbers and they walked over from Astoria or 125th Street or caught the bus. Simple transport for simpler days.

There had been lush grass in those days, too. Older players from some top European clubs remembered playing tour games there in the period after World War II when post-war visits were warmly attended by post-war immigrants, either there or at two now demolished fields, the Brooklyn Dodgers' home at Ebbets Field or the Polo Grounds, once looming across the river from Yankee Stadium. It was at Downing Stadium, too, that I recall the most original effort at crowd control when two teams from Central America were playing, in the mid 70s, and when a scuffle broke out on the field, scores of angry fans ran onto the field to join in. Repeated calls on the PA system for them to get back to their seats were of no avail until some bright spark made the announcement that if they didn't quit, the immigration service police would be called immediately. This sank in, after a couple of repetitions, and all was peaceful, again showing, if nothing else, that the current furor over illegal immigrants is nothing new.

You might ask: well, if Downing Stadium was so bad, why did you go there in the first place? The answer is that it was en route to Giants Stadium from Hofstra Stadium, where we had played for two years. Hofstra is way out on Long Island. Giants Stadium is way over in New Jersey. I did not want to stay at Hofstra and then, one day, make the gigantic hike away from a market in which we would then have played for five years and set up shop almost another world away. Downing Stadium, bad though it was, put us in the center of things, able to still touch our Long Island fans but be there, in the heart of the metropolitan area and a short jump to the Cosmos' eventual home.

Thinking of Downing Stadium makes me think of Sir Walter Scott (1771–1832), the great Scottish poet and novelist, author of *Ivanhoe* and *Rob Roy* among many others. He wrote a poem, turned into a tune, and sung plaintive and forlorn, about Clan McGregor, whose name was banned and lands taken from them for almost a century: We're landless, landless, landless Gregalach—Landless, landless, landless. And so were we.

There was not a single soccer stadium in the country, apart from a few fields with a few hundred bleachers in the deepest ethnic pockets of cities like New York and Chicago and Los Angeles. All the rest were baseball or American football stadia; the one with pitchers mounds, infield dirt and weird alignment, the other so narrow there was hardly room to swing a leg for a corner, never mind run up to it, and with endless markings on the field, causing confusion as to whether the ball was out of play or in or out of the penalty box. They had none of the aesthetics of our game—an almost untouched greensward, immaculately cut, crisply and minimally lined, perfectly rectangular, aligned with the stands, timeless, majestic and uplifting before even a player has set foot on it.

We were within touching distance of the first soccer-specific stadium in the mid-70s, a quarter of a century before Lamar Hunt built his in Columbus Ohio. We were going to take over Singer Bowl, once called Louis Armstrong Bowl, in Queens, New York where the National Tennis Center is now located and the US Open is played. It was then a neat little place, about the size of a hockey arena and the plan was to turn what was then the length into the width of a soccer field and elongate the whole thing to produce a 25,000-seat soccer stadium, ideally sized and ideally located. It fell through because the local community boards, which hold quite some power in New York City, protested, vociferously, when Warner executives went before them to set out the plans and Warner decided the public relations backlash wasn't worth the effort.

Chicago Sting in the 80s had an unique problem. Soldier Field, the previous home, was not available, so the Sting played at home at Comiskey Park, home of the White Sox, on the south side, and played at home at

Wrigley Field, home of the Cubs, on the north side. Not simultaneously, you understand, but at one or the other, depending on when the baseball teams were away and let us in. It's one thing to look at the schedule to see whether you are playing home or on the road; another entirely to see where you are playing at home from game to game. Although, when I went there, Mayor Bilandic had said, unequivocally, that there would be a domed stadium in the Windy City within three years, the wind still whistles through whatever they have there and it whistled so uncomfortably that even Lee Stern was ready to give up in 1980. He had me research every possible other landing place for the Sting, Jacksonville, Florida, Nashville, Tennesee and, mostly Milwaukee, Wisconsin. We had a deal on the table from Milwaukee, from a group ready to buy and play in County Stadium. But Lee's heart, as always, ruled his head and as his heart was in the Sting and in Chicago, he finally turned it down. And won two championships for his efforts, so I'm sure he is sure he made the right decision.

Soccer America asked many people, to celebrate their 20th anniversary in 1991—what would your magic wand give to American soccer? Twenty soccer stadia, about 15,000 to 25,000 seats, across the land, I replied. Amazingly, it is happening. But for us stadia was a running subject, running sore.

Our kinship with the aforementioned landless McGregors did not end there. Apart from losing their land, the poor souls also lost their name, it was "proscribed," could not be used, and here was our kinship coming to the fore again. The proper name of our game is Association Football, football for short and for all the world, except with different spellings like futebol and futbol and voessball. All the world except the US, and Canada, too, where football is that other truly silly game. In fact, the moment has come for me to say what I think about American football, a tiny riposte for all those ignorami who have taken aim at my game. I've been saving this. I hope you like it; well, anyway, I do.

The headline is below and if you love American football and do not want to be offended, please skip the next five paragraphs and then start again.

FINDING A NAME FOR NOTHING

The true story of an unfathomable American way of wasting time. Once upon a time in the land of Yale, there lived a man with nothing to do, so that is what he did—invented nothing. The brainwave came to him one day while watching a game of Rugby Football, a free-flowing game of passing and running and handling and tackling and tumultuous challenges for the ball, which itself had branched out from the game of Association Football which, of course, needs no introduction except to say it is the most sublime, nay divine, game; handed down by the true Gods.

While watching, he thought to himself . . . wait, wait, I can turn this into nothing, surely? And slowly, methodically, he did, sure in the knowledge that just as Pythagoras determined the sum of the square on the side opposite the hypoteneuse was equal to the sum of the squares on the other two sides, that the morons outnumbered those who were not brain dead by a similar ratio. So he produced this, er, event in which:

Large, mostly unfit men stand around for long periods of time having friendly chats. After running 10 or 20 yards, one of these large men will sit sucking oxygen for the rest of the day. Thereafter, a further conversation would take place, after which many large, unfit men, will crouch in positions in which, to borrow from Tom Hanks in the movie *Forrest Gump,* butt-ttocks would be the principal sight on view. Throughout the day, these events taking at least seven hours to conclude (except at a thing called the Super Bowl which begins on a Monday and ends three weeks after St. Crispin's Day), another group of men prance merrily among the large, mostly unfit men.

These are dressed in quite fetching stripes, with dinky little hats, and place their hands on their hips in provocative gestures or throw dainty little handkerchiefs in the air (no doubt hoping one of the larger men would pick it up and thus begin a conversation which might lead to, well, we blush at the thought). There was one problem the man in the land of Yale had to overcome—how to name this invention of nothing, hours and hours, in fact, of absolutely nothing, and then . . . and then . . . it happened.

One of the large, mostly unfit men (although he was not as large and maybe not as unfit as the rest) took the ball and . . . eureka . . . kicked it! Put his FOOT to the BALL. And because absolutely nothing else happened for all the many hours of the events past and the events future, that is why it came to be called FootBall. *Quod Erat Demonstrandum.* Walter Camp is the name of the man in the land of Yale. Look it up.

So we had to use our game's other name, used only in Britain and parts of the old Empire—soccer. That is not, as many believe, an Americanism. It was widely used when I was a boy in England and for long before that. It stems from the English habit of making some proper names, and people's names, more familiar than formal. Thus my late friend John Bromley, of TV fame in the UK, was Brommers; England's World Cup goalkeeper Gordon Banks was Banksie and so on. Thus Rugby Football, the handling game which broke from Association Football around the time of the American Civil War became rugger, from its first three letters, and as Association Football could not use its first three letters for the same purpose (go on, try it), it used letters 3 to 5 to make soccer.

It was wonderful, though, recently, to hear an American announcer on an American network say about an American team in an American league "They're playing some really good football." Attaboy, we'll get our name back, one day. Any lawyers out there want to help me sue the NFL? And before some very hard-working folk of the Randalls Island Foundation decide to sue me, let me say that times are a'changing and so is Randalls Island. Downing Stadium is gone, replaced by Icahn Stadium for track and field and as I am writing these words, plans are afoot (pun intended) to place a permanent marker to remember Pele. More than 30 soccer fields will open on Randalls Island. My suggestion is they're named Pele Fields and maybe by the time you read this, that will have happened.

Belo Horizonte, Brazil, in the World Cup of 1950. The United States has just beaten England 1-0 in a major upset and the goalscorer. Joe Gaetjens, is carried off by admiring Brazilian spectators. A sad fate awaited such a man.

MANHATTAN SOCCER CLUB, Inc.
INTERNATIONAL SOCCER LEAGUE
47 WEST 43rd STREET, NEW YORK 36, N.Y.

CABLE: MANSOCCER

NEW ADDRESS: CONNECTICUT SOCCER CLUB, INC.
100 Constitution Plaza
Hartford, Connecticut

Telephone MU 2-0944

WILLIAM D. COX
PRESIDENT

November 17, 1966

DWIGHT F. DAVIS
VICE PRESIDENT

ERNO SCHWARCZ
GENERAL MANAGER

Mr. Clive Toye
29 The Heights
Fox Grove Road
Beckingham, Kent
England

Dear Clive:

OFFICES ABROAD:

WALLEY BARNES
LONDON, ENGLAND

FRANK E. HOWELL
MADRID, SPAIN

SERGIO VASCONCELLOS
RIO DE JANEIRO, BRAZIL

JORGE P. ALMASQUE
LISBON, PORTUGAL

This letter will confirm my offer to you of a salary of $15,000
a year as Public Relations Director of the Connecticut Soccer
Club, Inc., 100 Constitution Plaza, Hartford, Connecticut.

To reiterate my verbal offer, I have listed below the items which
we have agreed upon.

1. The fares for yourself and dependents from London to
   Hartford, Connecticut, will be paid by the Connecticut
   Soccer Club, Inc.

2. A portion to be agreed upon of the cost of transporting
   furniture and personal effects will be paid by the
   Connecticut Soccer Club, Inc.

3. The Connecticut Soccer Club, Inc., will further give
   all assistance possible in the matters of visas, housing,
   and any other domestic problems that may arise.

I would want you to take up this permanent position in Hartford
at the earliest possible moment.

Sincerely,

William D. Cox

William D. Cox

WDC/rmu

The contract that lured me into this whole affair, from a club which never played
but from the man who started it all....William D. Cox (a one-time owner of the
Philadelphia Phillies).

KANSAS CITY'S FIRST
WORLD CUP
SOCCER MATCH

THE UNITED STATES WORLD CUP TEAM

Front row (left to right): James Benedek, Houston Stars; Willy Ray, Kansas City Spurs; Peter Millar, New York Inter; Mike Maliszewski, Baltimore Bays; Adolph Bachmeier, Chicago Mustangs; Carl Gentile, St. Louis Stars, and Joe Speca, Baltimore Bays. Back row: Victor Gerley, New York Ukrainians; Rusty Kindratiw, Balti-more Bays; Nick Krat, St. Louis Stars; Helmut Kofler, New York Gottschee; Bob Gansler, Chicago Mustangs; Emanuuel Abaunsa, Los Angeles Armenians; Larry Hausmann, Chicago Mustangs; Gary DeLong, Vancouver Royals, and Ed Clear, St. Louis Stars. Photo was taken before U. S. tied Israel, 3-3, in New York.

UNITED STATES vs. BERMUDA
1 p.m., Sunday, November 3, 1968
Municipal Stadium

25 cents

Hosted by

A US World Cup soccer match you could not see on TV, in a competition of which most Americans had never heard in a sport which so few played. It shows that American soccer, on its long journey to prominence, has come further in its trek than it still has to go.

Back in the dawn of US soccer…the 1967 Baltimore Bays, Eastern Division champions, losers to the Oakland Clippers in the championship game of the NPSL.

Randy Horton, now Minister of the Crown Colony of Bermuda, holds the Cosmos Championship pennant as if he dares anyone to think of taking it. On his right, Angelo Anastasio who was later to be released to make way for Pele on the roster.

Der Tag. Kaizer Franz ready to sign his contract, with Nesuhi Ertegun (standing center), then Chairman of the Cosmos, looking on.

The day of glory, when it was still all fun. The Cosmos locker room after our first championship win over St. Louis in 1972. Gordon Bradley, number 24 and coach, is in the middle. The Warner Communications ownership trio, Steve Ross, Jay Emmett, and Alan Cohen on the right.

Part of the courtship of Pele. He was playing for Santos against Deportivo Cali of Columbia in a doubleheader with us at Yankee Stadium. So I gave him a #10 Cosmos shirt and told him he would be wearing it one day. I'm not sure he believed me!

Gordon Bradley looks on as I hand Jorge Siega a memento of the fact that he was the very first player (and a very good one, too) to sign a Cosmos contract, for $75 a game.

The moment that was so unbelievable I can hardly remember a moment of it. Pele, in his Cosmos No. 10, entering the field at Downing Stadium, Randalls Island, to a thunderous welcoming, and changing everything. I know I was there, though, in the bottom left corner.

Franz Beckenbauer breaks into a smile as he signs his contract for the assembled media – for the umpteenth time!

Capturing the moment of Pele's 1250th goal was not to be missed. From the right – Gordon Bradley, Steve Ross, Pele, Jay Emmett and myself with Julio Mazzei in the front.

Oppostie page: Love, love, love. Pele saying goodbye to fans at Giants Stadium, goodbye to his days of playing but leaving us all with incomparable memories.

When the NASL folded, soccer did not fold; nor did our efforts to keep pushing it onward and upward. One big event at Giants Stadium was "The Legends...The Americas vs the Rest of the World" with Pele joining the promoters of Mundial Sports Group – Noel Lemon on the left and myself on the right.

Above: Roberto Bettega, one of the greatest of Italian goalscorers, played one night for Juventus in the final of the European Cup, signed, in Athens, the next day and gave cause for mirth when the Toronto media was brought in to hear about it.

Right: The day of induction into the US National Soccer Hall of Fame in 2003 with that great goalscorer, my grandson Cameron Jones, standing in front of me.

The Toronto Blizzard of the early 80s and what a fine team – with that excellent coach bob Houghton seated in the middle with two non-Americans who made the US Soccer Hall of Fame sitting on his right – Canadian Bruce Wilson and South African Ace Ntsoelengoe.

The locker room at Yankee Stadium the Pele scored his 1250th professional goal.
The inscription reads: "To My big boss from your friend Edson Pele."

13

NOT EVEN
GEORGE STEINBRENNER
HAS SAID ANYTHING
AS SILLY AS THIS

THE SILLIEST THING I ever said in my entire life was over the public address system at half-time at Yankee Stadium in the hearing of about 27,000 fans, two teams, one referee and two linesmen, league office officials, ushers, media, security, concessionaires and ball boys. In retrospect, it was dafter than anyone has ever said at Yankee Stadium, including the resident ogre, 'er, owner, George Steinbrenner and on a par with the utterances of peace and tranquility for all under the reign of the resident owner, 'er, ogre, Saddam Hussein, by Baghdad Iraq's Minister of Information as the tanks and footsloggers closed in on him.

"This is to advise you," I said "that the Cosmos will play not only the rest of the game but the rest of the season under protest." God knows what that meant then, or now, but it was the only way I could placate Steve Ross and stop him from telling the players not to go on the field for the second half. We were 3–1 down at half-time to the Tampa Bay Rowdies, the hated Tampa Bay Rowdies, and had two goals disallowed. Correctly disallowed, which didn't make me any happier, but there it was. I was up on the mezzanine level when Jay Emmett came rushing up saying I was needed urgently, Steve was going down to the locker room to tell the players to quit because he was so enraged at the disallowed goals. To this day I do not think I have heard anything quite so absurd, though that Iraqi Minister's statement that there were no US troops near Baghdad just as we saw a US tank nose its way round the corner and onto the screen, runs it close. In truth, his remarks would have run away with the first prize if it had not been for the fact that (a) he was a total moron, mouthing defense for a vicious tyrant and (b) I was not a total moron, mouthing words ordered by the Chairman of the Board of a famous US public company. Ponder that.

Anyway, down we rushed in a panic and there was Steve, and acolytes, pacing outside the locker room, fire in his eyes, steam coming from every pore and acolytes anxious to support him. I forget what I said or what he said or what anybody said but I know he agreed to let the game continue if I went on the PA and said the ridiculous things now printed above. I felt an idiot, though I have never yet had anyone say they heard me say it. Maybe no one listens to the PA properly, maybe I pushed the wrong button. So, we ended up winning 5–3 with a wonderful bicycle kick goal from Pele, maybe the most spectacular of his Cosmos goals, which is what people remember, not the stupid stuff they might have heard from me.

Steve Ross's inability to suffer disappointment boiled over on other occasions, too, and long after I left the club, Ted Howard recalls: "Steve Ross later threatened to pull the Cosmos not only out of a game but out of the league entirely . . . then just out of the playoffs, when we suspended Carlos Alberto because he went after the referee when the Cosmos lost in Vancouver. What a tirade." But if Steve Ross ever felt lonely when all games were not victories, every day was not shining with the rays of righteous, even regal, success, then companionship was on the way in the shape of Giorgio Chinaglia.

George (and I called him George often as time went by because he detested it, a residue of his unhappy years in South Wales, I imagine) was easy to sign. He spoke fluent English, with a trace of a Welsh accent from those young and very unhappy days in Swansea; he had an American wife, Connie, sister of the USA's hockey hero of the Olympics, Mike Eruzione, a home in New Jersey and nothing more he could do in Italy. On the plus side there, his goals had taken Lazio to their first Serie A title. On the negative side, he had been thrown off the national team after a bust-up with, and rude, public gesture at, the man in charge. For all the respect his goals earned him, he was not liked and no other club was pestering Lazio for his services. So, the USA it was for him.

He had shown how eager he was with a pack of lies in late '75, soon after we first talked of his coming to the Cosmos. He was on vacation, we could have done with some help and he, burrowing like a ferret for his target, had already latched on to Steve Ross and got a ride on the Warner jet to our game in Rochester. I was not on that trip but back in the office and from Rochester there came a succession of phone calls—from both Ross and Chinaglia, telling me that one or both had been on the phone to Lazio, at their offices in Rome, and that it was OK for him to play. It's all OK, they all said, he can play tonight; Lazio will lend him to us, we'll go down to the team meeting and tell Gordon to put Giorgio in the team tonight, right? No, it isn't right, I argued with both the player and the Boss of Bosses of Warner Communications. No, he can not play. We have no release from Lazio, we have no international clearance from the Italian FA, he can not, not, not play.

Well, that did not go down too well, believe me, not well at all but I followed up with the Italian authorities the next day and found it was a pack of lies. Lazio had not said he could sign on loan, the Italian FA knew nothing about it. I should have learned but I didn't. Here was a top Italian goalscorer, bilingual, from a good club with plenty of years and goals ahead of him and anxious to come. Too good to be true but true it was. I had some difficulty getting Lazio to sell him for a price I was prepared to pay and we had all manner of secret meetings and oblique glances and difficulty. But I offered $60,000 to Lazio, take it or leave it, and my friend Borje Lanz and I went to the final meeting, with suitcases deliberately packed and on view and Borje, who spoke good Italian, still pretending to speak no Italian.

We trundled into the Lazio office, plonked down our suitcases and said, with relaxed smiles, that we could not leave Rome without saying goodbye, so here we were and could they phone for a taxi to take us to Fiumicino? Someone was on the phone to President Lenzini in short order and Borje was easily able to understand their panicked "they are on the way to the airport!!!" remarks and enable us to stay calm and disinterested and be persuaded to wait for the President to arrive, and he did and the deal was done. Giorgio made a meal of his departure as he tried desperately to puff up his importance, as if he didn't have enough self-importance in any case, and went to the trouble of building up and paying for his own "secret" departure, including renting his own private plane (because he knew we had provided one for Pele) and letting the Italian media know so he could be photographed in such splendor. So we had provided Pele with a private plane for his arrival and Franz with a helicopter in from JFK but would have happily supplied George with an economy class ticket on any airline he chose. The Chinaglia deal was cheap, although it cost the Cosmos millions later when he gained influence over Ross and spending. That influence, that relationship between the two men, caused great concern and curiosity then and continues to mystify today. Years later Jay Emmett, who as one of the executives in what was called Office of the President, was a lot closer to Ross than I was, asked me: What was it with Giorgio and Steve? I do not know. But it was not normal.

Gordon Bradley remembers: "I was in Steve Ross's office, having a quiet chat, and the door opened and in came Chinaglia, no knock, no nothing, and he walked around behind Steve's chair, grabbed a bottle of Chivas Regal, poured himself a glass and just sat down. Not a word, no hello, no asking if it was OK to have a drink. Nothing. And Steve said nothing." On the other hand, on several occasions when Ross asked for a meeting about the team with Gordon and myself, and later with Ken Furphy, too, when Ross insisted I fire Gordon (so I moved him upstairs and hired Ken as coach), we found Chinaglia already in the room, to become part of the debate. Truly bizarre. As Werner Roth once asked: Is Giorgio having his own private elevator built to the 32nd floor, so he can get up to see Steve easily?

Mark Ross, Steve's son, later described Chinaglia as "like a second father to me. My own father had the best time of his life with the Cosmos, it was a wonderful experience being with him then." Not for everyone, of course. Another one over whom George held sway for the longest time was Peppe Pinton, fellow Italian, local soccer official in Connecticut, rising in the end to become one of the last General Managers, under President Chinaglia, but the time came when Peppe unloaded to me on years of thought about George:

> "Giorgio was born to destroy things. He would be ready to tear his hair out every day if he could not think of something vindictive to do to someone he thought didn't like him. He would go into Rafael's office or mine and say, very confidentially, look I have just come from Steve and he says so and so has to go or something like that and everyone was frightened and sure that word had come from Steve. Giorgio told me to give some of the players a lot more money—so they would be on his side—and I did so. I thought orders had come from Steve. Then at a board meeting, they asked: Who authorized all this? And what could I say" I did. So Ahmet said you're fired.

"At the very end, I was at the Tre Scalini with Giorgio and he said, don't worry, Steve will take of you and he picked up the phone and dialed Steve's private number at home and told him: we have to take care of Peppe. So, I went in to see Ed Aboudi about my deal and they said there was no such thing. Steve had never heard of it. So I realized what had been happening all along, much of the time. . . . Giorgio had been phoning his own home and having a conversation with his own telephone. He hadn't been speaking to Steve at all. Not then, and not many times before."

But 1976 wasn't all silly remarks at Yankee Stadium and The Days of Steve and George. We had not one but two Pele tours, one before the season and one after, which were not only profitable but hard work to arrange, hard work to undertake and hard work on our prize, Pele. I recall Pele, on arrival in Antwerp on the start of the post-season Cosmos tour, when presented with the list of media and public appearances I wanted him to do: "Clivey, you make me work too hard." And I did. My normal practice was to present him with a list about five times longer than what I really wanted him to do, then negotiate down to the real needs. It always worked.

Pele, by the way, was not alone in never being able to call me Clive, just one syllable. The Portuguese and Spanish languages call for all letters to be pronounced, so the "e" on the end of mine is there to be spoken. Cost me an important phone call at Barajas airport, Madrid, once when the operator was paging Clibay Toyay. What I must have been called at the end of that tour, however, is still a mystery, though I can guess at the words used, having used them all myself from time to time.

We had started in Paris, then Antwerp and thence to Japan, via Abu Dhabi and Bombay, for one game in Osaka and the last one in Tokyo where some enterprising soccer shoe salesmen gathered the players together, without my knowledge, gave them free shoes and the promise of $100 if they wore them the next day against the Japanese national team. I knew nothing about this until alerted by the bustle of activity and noise in the corridor outside my room, with doors being knocked and boxes of shoes being trundled up and down. What's all this then, I asked? On being told, I said not bloody likely. For a start, you're not wearing shoes you have never even tried on before in a game against the national team with the Crown Prince present and, for an end, the club has a shoe deal, with Pony. So, no.

Dark mutterings and then a phone call from the captain, Werner: The players are having a meeting down here and want you to come down to discuss this, he said. No, I said, I'm going out for dinner. Well, we won't play then, said Werner. So, have a nice trip, I said, I have your return tickets. So the game was played and all returned home on those tickets, except Chinaglia. He didn't want to fly the long way home, via Europe, with the team, including the greatest player of all time, so he bought his own ticket across the Pacific. It was about this time that he came in to renegotiate his three-year contract which was for about $40,000 a year. No, I said, that's it. So with a smirk he said "no problem, I'll go and see Steve."

But there was still the future and the fun to stop us being too distracted by the Steve and George Show. First, there was the first flirtation and growing romance with Franz Beckenbauer, for whom great praise as a person and as a professional is well deserved, though his impending arrival was not universally welcome, the ambivalence coming through in the remark of Seattle Sounders' owner Walt Daggett, on hearing my next signing was to be Beckenbauer: "I don't know whether to thank you or to curse you." Second, there was the continuing fun and frolic of people who didn't always take themselves seriously.

Werner Roth continues the saga of Pedro Garay: "I was having a rub down on the table before the game in Vancouver when I felt Pedro pulling my arm up into the air and then the feel and sound of handcuffs being put on one wrist; some of the lads had put him up to it. He then tried to grab my other arm to put on the other cuff when I try to push him away, look up and see this terrible blank expression come over his face as he turns away and runs out of the locker room and doesn't come back. So here I am with a cuff on my wrist and the chain and the other cuff dangling down, so we tape it all up to my arm and tell the referees that it's a sprain or something and on the field we go.

"We are lining up for the national anthems when the door from the locker rooms bursts open and there is Pedro, being tackled and dragged by security guards all over him and as they are trying to pull him down, he throws something on to the field and yells "the keys." What had happened was this. Obviously he had forgotten that he had left the keys back in his hotel room, so he had gotten in the car and driven back to the hotel. That didn't take him long because all the traffic was coming towards the stadium, it was a Pele game, so when he started back he ran into traffic and trouble. The stadium was right next to a huge amusement park, something like Six Flags, and Pedro could see the stadium in the distance over all the rides. So he abandons his car and sets off at a run towards the amusement park and the stadium, about four miles away. He runs through the amusement park and then gets to a 15-foot fence separating it from stadium property, which he proceeds to climb over, with security people now on the alert and chasing him . . . then he runs past the lines of cars and people at the turnstiles and jumps over the turnstiles, because he doesn't have time to explain, so more security people join the chase, before he bursts past security at the locker rooms and just manages, disheveled and out of breath, to throw the keys before they all pile on him and take him away."

For a security man, Pedro certainly had his run-ins with security men as Steve Marshall, our large, indeed sometimes larger than life, traveling secretary remembers:

> "Pedro was running, following Pele off the field, but his official ID got stuck under his coat, so one of the stadium security guys just thumped him, and we had live TV interviews in the locker room with Pedro sitting there in plain view with an ice bag on his head."

Pedro's fellow countryman, Rafael de la Sierra, was not the least excitable person in the Cosmos menagerie, to put it mildly. He was a nice enough fellow, an architect by profession, and sucked, bit by bit, into the obsession. So much so that he came up with a novel way of trying to beat the loathed Tampa Bay Rowdies. Mix laundry liquid in Gatorade, leave it in the visitors' locker room and somewhere just after half time, they should be running for the toilets, hoping at least they get off the field in time. Sounded like a fine idea but on the grounds of poor sportsmanship, I would not let him do it. In any case, it might not have worked.

Poor Rafa, he must have suffered the flames of hell the day he and a group of lawyers and accountants had been sent on their own to Santos to meet with Pele and his helpers, back in 1975; the only meeting I didn't attend in the whole saga. Jay Emmett had called me in the middle of the night to say everything had gone wrong, the lawyers were threatening to fight each other and we needed to meet first thing to try to solve it. We shouldn't have sent boys to do a man's job, was how he put it. In those days, it took hours to get an international call, hours from almost anywhere, to almost anywhere, so a call had been booked in the early hours of the morning to come through to Jay's office at 11 a.m., by when we would have worked out what to do and what to say about the conflagration in the night. So the call came through and we talked Rafael and the others through the words and tactics to be used and at the end Jay said: "And remember, Rafael, remember at all costs that the most important thing of all is . . ."

And then he hung up, laughed and said: "He'll be going frantic down there all day, trying to get back to me, can you imagine it? It'll take him hours, if he ever gets through and I won't take his call if he does get through. It'll drive him mad." We enjoyed that.

Ted Howard adds to those memories: "There was a bad relationship between the federation and many of the clubs and on one occasion, the USSF wanted to use Giants Stadium for a national team game, which was a difficult issue because the Cosmos had exclusivity for soccer. So we arranged a meeting between Rafael and an USSF delegation, including the President, Gene Edwards, and the General Secretary, Kurt Lamm, and the people from the league, the intermediaries, myself included, met with Rafael first and said—look, just take it easy, listen to what they have to say and then we'll talk about and see if we can come to the right decision. Well, Rafael said that was fine and in came the USSF people. They started to make their case and within a minute, no more, Rafael leaped to his feet screaming, screaming at them at the top of his voice, calling them all the names under the sun and ordering them out of his office. End of meeting."

14

GONE AND SOON FORGOTTEN, AND NOT ONLY ME

IT WAS THE best of times, it was the worst of times. Charles Dickens, in whose favorite pub, the Cheshire Cheese, I often lunched in my Fleet Street days, began his *Tale of Two Cities* with those lines but I'm borrowing them to tell my story of one city (plus that bit of New Jersey where New York teams have to play because there's nowhere for them in New York) in the year of 1977.

This is how romantic and exciting the NASL was in the 70s. Lawrie Mifflin, one of the Cosmos media corps, was offered the baseball job on the *New York Times;* one of the plum jobs in sports reporting. She asked me what I thought she should do. Do you want bylines from Tokyo and Paris, I said, or from Cleveland and Detroit? She never did cover baseball for the NYT. The media friendly Cosmos, well at least we tried to be, allowed the media to come into the locker rooms 10 minutes after the game. So, I said to Lawrie Mifflin, of the *New York Times* and the female sex (and not to be confused with that superbly skilled but wayward Peruvian mid-fielder we signed from Santos, Ramon Mifflin):

I seem to remember you were the first to break the barrier, enter the unknown and turn the world upside down, the first person of the opposite gender to intrude into the male domain of the locker room. How, why, when, where did that happen and what do you have to say for yourself, you brazen hussy?

Lawrie explained:

"Inevitably it was going to happen. Women were interested in sports, women were becoming journalists, so it was only a matter of time.

When I went to Yale, in 1969, it was the first time they took women undergraduates and coming from Philadelphia where women's sports were popular I went along innocently and asked to sign up for the women's field hockey team. They looked at me in amazement but eventually this led to a whole series of women's teams but the student newspaper refused to send anyone to cover them, so I did. Then, when I was on the news desk of the *Daily News,* I noticed that the Queens College women's basketball team was one of the best in the country, but we didn't cover them, so I did, and then in the 1976 Olympics, women's basketball was included for the first time, so I was sent to Montreal to cover that and the rest of the Games. When I came back, as hockey was low man on the totem pole, and possibly because the *Times* had a woman covering the Islanders, I was given the New York Rangers to cover and that was the first time I was allowed into the locker room . . . followed in the 1977 season by being the first into a soccer locker room.

"Of course, I took to soccer right away, it is so similar to field hockey, and I fell in love with it, how could you not fall in love with the Cosmos. I remember the Cosmos bought bathrobes for all the players—and a bathrobe or a towel round the waist was enough, locker rooms are not the most sexual situations—and the media thought that was very classy of the Cosmos. I never had a problem in a soccer locker room, though I had a few in hockey. The players were unfailingly polite—though I remember Paul Gardner saying to Jim Trecker outside the locker room—you're not letting her in there! The next year Helene Elliott came to *Newsday* from Chicago, so there were two of us. It all passed off very easily and naturally."

Not much else did. There were the minor hiccups, of course. Having previously hired the assistant PR director of the New York Jets (the aforementioned James Trecker, who went on to stardom as head of the 1994 World Cup PR machine), I went and hired their assistant GM Mike Martin. "Soon after you hired me as GM in '77," recalls Mike, "I joined the team in Bermuda where they were in training. A day after I arrived the team had a friendly match with the Bermuda national side. I joined the Bermuda Football Association officials and both sides on the pitch prior to the start of the match. To my horror I found that one of my duties was to introduce each Cosmos player to the Bermuda officials. At that time I hadn't met all the players myself. So I stood there red faced in obvious distress when Captain Keith Eddy, realizing my predicament, quickly came over and went down the line introducing each player and saved the day. During that same training session in Bermuda we played a friendly match against the Bermuda Under 21 side. The game was scheduled on a practice pitch late one muggy afternoon. The first half was decidedly one-sided with the Cosmos ahead something like 6–0. It started to rain in the second half and then it poured. It came down in buckets. But the match continued until scores of frogs, huge, massive frogs, started to emerge from the turf. By then we were ahead 11–0 and both sides agreed to suspend the match. The only match in soccer history, possibly, where the result was: Game abandoned, Frogs."

This is how the deliberate animosity of many media showed itself up to be moronic. Frank Deford, a well-known US writer and broadcaster (though considering his turgid prose, I can not understand why), did a TV piece saying: The most ridiculous play in all of sport is the penalty kick in soccer. Then he showed tape of a free kick from outside the box.

And again. Prescott Sullivan in the San Francisco *Examiner* wrote: "In Europe as in South America they go raving mad over the game. Pray that it doesn't happen here. The way to beat it is constant vigilance and rigid control. If soccer shows signs of getting too big, swat it down." They were not alone. Dick Young, New York *Daily News* sports editor and columnist and all-round man of influence in those days, once said to one of his young reporters: "Don't waste your time on soccer, young man; it's a game for Commie pansies." A game for Commie pansies. Go on, say it again. From what depths of Neanderthal mindlessness did that emerge? Yet the man was a renowned sports editor of a major metropolitan newspaper.

Yet there were the converts, the young, articulate, intelligent ones who were often sent to cover soccer because they were lowest on the totem pole and who grew to like, even love, the game and enjoyed the refreshing openness and friendliness of soccer people and soccer players in contrast to the athletes and people in other American sports. People like Dave Hirshey and Lawrie Mifflin, Alex Yannis and the perennial Paul Gardner, Ike Kuhns and others in New York, Mike Conklin in Chicago, Jeff Lebow and Jim Kernaghan in Toronto, Jim Karvellas, who watched his first soccer game with me in the broadcast booth for WJZ in Baltimore and became the voice of both the Cosmos and the Knicks, John Miller and Bob Carpenter who went on to TV fame in other sports . . . they all gave us and the game a fair shot. Pity is that most of them, and others around the nation, were too talented to stay in sports, or at least our sport. So they went off in other directions and were lost to the game, as were so many bright young men and women within the League and club offices.

I have still not been able to fathom the built-in antipathy, antagonism to soccer from the so-called mainstream media or why people were sent to cover it, or write about from afar, with disdain and with malice afore-thought. After all, is someone who does not like opera sent to cover opera? Would a philistine like me be sent to cover the ballet? Would any-one let me, please, write about American football? No, it is routine that people with at least an alleged knowledge of the subject are sent to cover that event, routine, except with the US media and soccer. A man named John Arlott, a famed cricket writer in days gone by, once said that to cover a sport properly you needed to be "in sympathy with the game." Not a shill, like so many show biz journalists; not hired by the club to do TV play-by-play or color "and be careful what you say." No, simply have a feeling for what you are about to see and say it is good or it is bad on its merits. Pat McBride, stalwart of the St. Louis Stars thought so too: The St Louis *Post* would always send a reporter who had never played and couldn't even kick a ball. It would have been nice to have been covered by someone who had a passion for the game.

I did actually cover one American football game in the distant past, at White City in London between two US Military teams, one from Ger-many and one from England. It was stupefyingly boring and the assem-bled media looked at each other with raised eyebrows and pained expres-sions. But we were not experts on the game we were writing about, we had no idea what was being done, or why, so we wrote kindly of the color and atmosphere and the look on the faces and sound of the voices of the few thousand American expatriates who were there enjoying themselves. I am sure no one poured scorn on the game nor wrote of 35,000 empty seats. A baseball game on a Tuesday night can draw a few thousand people and that goes unremarked. A soccer game at the same time was likely to be described as playing before 50,000 empty seats. A hundred thousand soccer games can be played around the world on a given weekend and somewhere a score of so of fans will misbehave . . . reported thus in the *New York Times,* for sure (well, they have to get their facts right sometime) and countless other organs of the Fourth Estate. The answer lies alongside those other great conundrums of human life like where do flies go in the wintertime or what happens to those socks which disappear in the washing machine so you're left with a drawer full of odd ones or why do massive traffic holdups appear on the highways for no apparent reason, no accident, no road works and then clear just as mysteriously. Answers are anxiously sought, especially about the socks.

It is also sad and true that American efforts in soccer have been largely mocked by the media overseas and I have a theory for that, too. Any Great Power will have its fair share of jealousy or enmity spread around the world. It was so when Britain was itself a Great Power and it is so now that the USA is one, so anyone with a touch of jealousy or enmity is going to write in that vein. But, and it is a big but, that criticism must necessarily be about American ways, American products, American thought and then, suddenly, here they are doing "our" thing, playing "our" game, something we actually know about, so what an easy target. We can be contemptuous about American soccer because while we don't know America, even though we are jealous of it, we do know soccer and thus our barbs must surely be truly aimed and our poison delivered to the target with enough venom to spread into other parts of that body. There was, and is, a certain amount of fear built into it, too, as if the underlying thought, not quite expressed, is: "oh God, please don't let them be good at that, too." There has been, in total, more absolute rubbish, total drivel, written and spouted at home and abroad about American soccer than about all other sports of the world for all time.

But, I digress. Here we are in 1977 and Giants Stadium is the mecca of US soccer, right? Cosmos Country. Carly Simon singing *Nobody Does It Better* as the glittering dust rains down from the upper level. Venue for the 1994 World Cup. Well, Sonny Werblin must have had such a vision when he oversaw the construction of the facility and insisted it was built wide enough for soccer, instead of narrow like traditional American football fields. Not so Steve Ross. He was against the move to Giants Stadium because, he said there was no subway. It was no good pointing out that habitation of the new refurbished Yankee Stadium was well-nigh impossible . . . the Yankees had the right to cancel any or all of our games there up to three hours before the kickoff if they felt that the field was too wet or rain was likely—or they thought that rain might be likely. One year of that was murder; waiting until 4 pm on a weekday, 11 am on a Sunday, to see which plan of action to be put into effect. Play—or tell 15,000–20,000 people to go home. We used to wait with real tension, waiting for the message and rushing to put game organization into effect when it didn't arrive.

I don't know on what point I won that battle—but I am sure it cost me in the future. As did another battle with the Brothers Ertegun. They didn't want Franz Beckenbauer. Another battle won with wounds not recognized at the time. It was impossible to win accord from both factions—the Ross/Warner faction and the Ertegun faction. It wasn't friendly and it wasn't fun. Everyone knows about what is often called the Bronx Zoo, lorded over by The Boss, George Steinbrenner. Imagine dealing with not one man but with a group like that. The opposition to Franz was about money, I think. Not so with a goalkeeper called Errol Yasin. We were just about ordered by the Erteguns to sign him, then were castigated for not paying him enough money. So they gave him more from one of their record company accounts. The Erteguns, as I mentioned, were Turkish. So, surprise, surprise, was Errol Yasin.

Once signed, they wanted him to play instead of Shep Messing, American, of some talent (most of which he displayed in the centerfold of the magazine *Playgirl*). So, many times more than once, you could have seen a brigade of executives—Ross and Emmett and Ertegun and Ertegun and de la Sierra and Toye and whomever else, leaving 75 Rockefeller Plaza in several limousines, to go to the East Side Heliport and 'copter across to Giants Stadium to sit down with Gordon Bradley to have a huge argument about whether Shep or Errol played in goal. Read again and weep. But it is true. Nothing much of importance could have been happening within Warner Communications that day though Ted Ashley, Chairman of Warner Bros, called me once "Thanks Clive." For what, I asked? "Thanks for the Cosmos, for taking Steve's attention, now I can make movies."

The first soccer event at Giants Stadium also saw an event unique in the annals of world football. We had a four-team tournament—Cosmos, Tampa Bay, Toronto and the champions of Haiti, Victory FC. Leaving the field, the players would go down the tunnel behind one goal and turn left into the locker room area. At half-time, most of the Victory players failed to take a left turn, preferring to walk straight ahead, out of the stadium, through the private parking lot and through the wire where their compatriots were waiting with raincoats to put over their uniforms and cars to transport them to a new life. Immigration made easy. Emigrating from Haiti to the USA always was, and is, damned difficult. Neither the law nor the authorities care if boatloads of Cubans set foot in Florida but Haitians? That's a different matter. Anyway, at half-time we did not have enough players for Victory to play the second half. So one of our local Haitian friends went on the public address system and, in Creole, so no one else ever got the message, asked a number of players from local Haitian-American League clubs to get to the locker room, toute de suite. Bless their hearts, enough answered the call and changed hastily and played.

This was also the day we honored members of the US Soccer Hall of Fame, those old codgers who had kept the flame flickering, and the day one of them died happy. We had them all take up playing positions in one half of the field and introduced them all and Pele ran round to each one, shook their hands and said thank you. A few days later, the daughter of one of them, Eric Charleson, rang me to say her father had died at night when he returned home from Giants Stadium. I expressed my sympathy but she replied that it was okay. Her father had called on the way home and said it was the happiest day of his life, to see such a crowd, to see soccer played in such a stadium and to be thanked by Pele. "So he died happy," she said.

By early summer, as the crowds poured in, so did Steve Ross's enthused entourage of acolytes grow and of all the acolytes, I think the prize must go to Allie Sherman, one-time coach of the New York Giants and a man of so little, so little, well, anything that, to my mind, he displaced no air when entering a room. Acolyte Allie was offered to me by Steve as a candidate for general manager and after a long conversation I came to the inescapable conclusion to that have him anywhere near the Cosmos would be an unmitigated disaster. (Right there, Toye). So, as gently as I could I told Steve, as politically correct as I could, that Acolyte Allie was not right for the job and was probably overqualified (Wrong move there, Toye). So Acolyte Allie was hired by Steve Ross and placed somewhere in between Warner and me. His outstanding contribution to the welfare and progress of the Cosmos stays in my mind to this day. He came, this little man from New York with the acquired Southern accent and way of trying to make himself look tough, and said we had to liven up the way we started the games. Get all the players in the center circle, he said. Have Pele juggle the ball for a couple of minutes, then Beckenbauer for a couple of minutes, then the rest of them, one by one. Wrong, Allie, I said. Pele and Beckenbauer are the greatest in the world and I am not turning them into Harlem Globetrotters. And, as for the rest of them, they couldn't juggle the ball for two minutes if you paid them. I forgot the fact that even if you used only the starting lineup, that's 22 minutes of juggling.

Butchers, too, can be dangerous, especially when you feed them something you shouldn't. I found that out when one of the newly obsessed Warner execs (one of those who six months earlier didn't know the shape of the ball and who was now eagerly listening to every word from his leader's lips—that's Steve Ross, not me) heard the name Frank Backenhauer or something like that and the Cosmos were going to sign him, they hoped. Mrs. Newly Obsessed Exec went to the local branch of the well-known German-American butcher, Karl Ehmer, and hearing the accent and guessing he might be interested, told him that the Cosmos were going to sign this famous German guy, Frank something-or-other. It didn't take the butcher long to work out who she was talking about and he told Karl Scheibock, the reporter for the then still-flourishing German language paper *Staats Zeitung und Herold* and Karl had the first and only world exclusive in his life. Much as I hated to do so, I denied it because I never did believe in lying to the media because you are, then, lying to your public. I always said that, as in a court of law, you tell the media the truth and nothing but the truth—but ignore the court requirement to tell the whole truth and I tried to live by that. But here it was either laugh and obfuscate or lose Beckenbauer, negotiations with whom were reaching a late stage, meaning it was basically agreed and now the lawyers and accountants were to earn their pay. Secrecy was vital and Karl its victim. After all, I had been living under an assumed name at the Hotel Vierjahrszeiten in Munich. I had been picked up in one speeding Mercedes on a prearranged corner, not far from where they shot Hitler in the 30s, though not badly enough, and then deposited in a lonely spot in the woods. Picked up there by another speeding Mercedes and taken to the forest home of a friend of Franz's, a couple totally unconnected with the club or football.

There we'd talk—Franz, his agent Robert Schwann, who was also general manager of Bayern Munich (what's German for conflict of interest?) and Bayern Munich coach Dettmar Cramer. As an aside, Dettmar was at one time head of coaching for the United States Soccer Federation. He quit over money. Not money for himself, that was available, but money to hold all the seminars and clinics and practical things he wanted and needed to do if his job was worthwhile. "I don't want to be paid just to sit in an office in the Empire State Building" was his unusual and admirable reason for quitting. Anyway, all that secrecy led to the Butcher, the Cover Up and then the Agreement. (Mike Martin recalls he was in my office when I took a phone call from Schwann confirming the deal was done. "You put the phone down and said—f . . . g hell, what have I done?")

It needed, for tax reasons, to be signed in Switzerland. It seemed as if every sentence from Schwann ended in the word "steuer." It means taxes. Robert was busy as a bee flitting, tax wise, between Kitzbuhel in Austria and Sarnen in Switzerland, trying to keep "steuer" at a minimum but you know what they say about death and taxes. Much later on the authorities found a flaw somewhere and down came the might of the law upon them, or at least a reasonable facsimile thereof. So, hiding still behind another name (I should have been prepared for this, in the Army I was in a force they called the Cloak and Dagger Boys), I booked a room and a conference room at a hotel in Lausanne and flew to Zurich and drove down. Franz and his retinue drove directly there from Munich and entered through the back door in disguise. We went up to the second floor conference room and laid out over this huge table all the many copies of the many documents we had to sign. All in private, all in secret and we started to do the signing.

I do not know what made me look up and out of one of the large picture windows. But there, on the other side of the street, the narrow, Swiss street, was another building, out of whose windows opposite our floor hung, festooned like gargoyle, about a score of press photographers, busily catching the moment of truth for the Kaizer and the Cosmos. When Franz finally arrived in New York, we were at another important meeting the night of the great New York blackout, when all power failed, the city was in total darkness for hours and we had to walk up, and down 23 flights of stairs in the hotel in the pitch black. We could have done with that blackout in Lausanne. And when Franz finally arrived in New York, we drummed up a group of boys in soccer uniform from the Cosmopolitan Junior League and they met him at JFK, with a huge welcoming banner. Standing right next to Franz behind the banner was a little lad who 14 years later was captain of the US national team in the 1990 World Cup in Italy, Mike Windischmann by name. Often in the stands watching in those days, and sometimes playing in preliminary kids games, were some others who later wore the national team shirt with distinction—Tony Meola, John Harkes, Claudio Reyna and Tab Ramos. We may have gone, but the influence lingers on.

Another agreement had been scribbled on the back of an envelope, resting on the top of a very dusty car late one night outside the stadium in Santos. (One, by the way, they hardly ever used in their glory days, it was a small, ill-maintained, wreck of a place and Santos preferred the huge modern stadium in Sao Paulo; not to mention the money the crowds brought in, of course). Anyway, there we were, yours truly and the President of Santos, a nice old chap called Modesta Roma. It was spring time in 1975 and the signing of Pele looked by now as if it really was going to happen. "I envy you," he said. "I wish he was staying." So, on the spur and emotion of the moment, I said I would give him back to Santos at the very end, for one half, the last half of his life. We scribbled the agreement there and then, on the back of an envelope, resting on the top of a very dusty car late one night outside the stadium in Santos. A fee of $20,000, travel and hotel expenses and a final game at Giants Stadium, Cosmos vs Santos, with Pele changing shirts at half time.

By the time it happened, three years later, the world had turned upside down and that game was a worldwide TV event, with people hanging from the rafters at Giants Stadium, Pele running around shouting Love Love Love—and scoring his last goal, too, a quickly taken free kick when he noticed the wall shift fractionally and belted it around the edge. I wish he had gone on forever. But, then, so does everyone else who ever saw him play and those football people who never saw him play are the unluckiest people in the world.

By the time it happened, on worldwide TV, in front of 78,000 adoring fans (well, about 76,000 adoring fans and the glitterati of New York in attendance) I was gone, too. I still had a three-year consulting contract, use of my office and my private box at Giants Stadium, but I was gone, fired the day after we put 62,000 into Giants Stadium in a game against the Minnesota Kicks. I was able to use my private box for that final game, the game I had thought of, the drama I had imagined, but that was all. The parties, the receptions, the field before the game were littered with people who had nothing at all to do with it, or the game of soccer—Mohammad Ali, Frank Gifford, for Christ's sake, and all the acolytes and hangers-on and lackeys; but yours truly was already a nonperson. My departure caused a bit of a storm for a few months and I still have some of the letters from fans and writers and personalities saying nice things about me and nasty things about the brass at Warner.

Vince Barraco of the Long Island Junior League wired the New York media: "Clive Toye's removal is an affront to the people of New York." Julius Alonso wrote on behalf of the New York and New Jersey members of the US Hall of Fame (glad to be with you, there in the Hall, Julius, will catch up with you elsewhere one of these days, keep a seat for me). Pete Dalebrook, manager at Hofstra Stadium when we played there, wrote about Warner's worst move. Dave Hirshey, once of the *Daily News* but on to greater things in magazines and publishing, wrote the nicest six paragraphs any journalist ever wrote about me, ending by writing: "You probably couldn't hear it, but the people at Giants Stadium were chanting "Thank you, Clive, thank you, Clive. The sentiment was nice but the message was better. They weren't saying thanks for the memories. They were saying thanks for the future." Paul Zimmerman wrote a column in the New York *Post* starting: The man who planned the Cosmos miracle in the Meadows wasn't around to see it Sunday night. Jerry Izenberg's piece in the Newark *Star Ledger* was headed: Crazy Clive will rise again (Jerry had always said I was crazy to think of doing the things I was doing). And then from Bob Hermann, Chairman of the Executive Committee: "You have given more to the success of soccer in the United States than any single other person in the league. You will be greatly missed."

A few weeks before Pele's farewell game, when we—sorry, they—won the championship by beating Seattle in Portland, Cynthia Kingdon, our long-time secretary wrote: "As I was waiting down at the locker room after the game, I suddenly realized that I was on the verge of tears. They were not tears of joy but more tears of sadness. Winning the championship should have been one of the great joys of my life but somehow I felt robbed of that feeling. I glanced around in confusion and realized that it was because I didn't have the two people there to hug and share the joy who deserved it . . . you and Gordon." Yes, Gordon Bradley, reinstated by then, had gone, too, unprotected when I left and his endless, selfless labor cast aside because Chinaglia wanted Eddie Firmani from Tampa Bay, someone whom he could manipulate and control. Not like Gordon.

As Mike Martin again recounted:

> "The whole thing began to disintegrate when you had gone, no rudder left, no one to protect the club. One order would be countermanded by someone else. Ahmet Ertegun had met Krikor Yepremian, the brother of Garo, the NFL kicker, by chance in the Waldorf, so he was hired by the Erteguns. So he was general manager at one end of the office and I was general manager at the other end and when I heard Ahmet and Krikor speaking at length in Turkish, I knew my days were numbered."

Gone, too, were a couple of projects, one being Flight 10, the Odyssey of Pele. It never happened. It was to be his farewell, a charter flight which I arranged through TWA and one final game on each continent. Wild idea, said the Warner brass. Ridiculous. Luckily, they must not have been paying too much attention when all those other ridiculous ideas were put into action—like Pele, Beckenbauer and the World Cup. Some of those final Pele games did happen, including the People's Republic of China, where the Cosmos became the first US professional sports team to visit after the start of the Nixon-Kissinger thaw. But ideology still ruled. Once I had finished with all the complicated negotiations, with help from George Bush, long before he became President of course, the documentation over visas began.

The Chinese authorities in Washington DC approved all except one. "He is a representative of the racist government in South Africa. We will not permit him to enter," they said. Yes, I said, but the racist government in South Africa is white, are you not supposed to be helping the oppressed blacks? "Yes, so he can not enter." Look at his photo, I said, he's black, one of those you say you are trying to help. "He can not enter," they said. So, Jomo Sono, one of the great ones and now the corpulent, affluent owner of the Jomo Cosmos, stayed home. But despite it all, the changes had happened and looking back I suppose it was inevitable. The whole thing had become much too big and important and glamorous for this hireling, yours truly, to be in charge; to be seen to be in charge; to get his face in the papers; to visit the President in the White House and all that kind of stuff. The ownership itself was in warring factions over the Cosmos—the true soccer fans, well, Nesuhi for sure and to some extent Ahmet Ertegun, largely to protect his nicer brother, on the one side, Steve Ross, egged on by the egregious Chinaglia, and his followers on the other. (My wife once overheard a fan approach Nesuhi and thank him for all that he had done. Nesuhi pointed to me and said "that's the man you should thank, he's the one who did it." Such generosity of spirit came from no one else and not, after a while from even Nesuhi.)

There were new employees being flung at me from all quarters, sons-in-law and someone's kids' tutor, looking for summer work, and the future Mrs. Ross. It was total bloody chaos and I said so; either run it the way I have run it for six-and-a-half years or. . . ? So Jay Emmett called me up to his office, closed and locked the door and said: "Okay, its chaotic downstairs, so we're here to settle your contract. You can keep your Warner options and get a three-year consulting contract." That was it but at least it was straightforward and it wasn't Jay's doing. In fact years later he asked me "why did you leave the Cosmos." I replied: "Because you fired me you silly bugger."

But what was to follow was truly the measure of men, the petty measure of men with wealth and power and glory within their own businesses; enough, you would have thought for anyone. No, they then had to rewrite history by eliminating my name from all Cosmos literature, current and historical, and even air-brushing me out of all photographs of the famous moments with Pele and Beckenbauer and all. Sad, really, sad for them that they had to stoop so low. But if you want to look at my passport, and theirs, you can see who was commuting to Sao Paulo and Santos and Guaruja and Frankfurt and Munich and Rome and god knows where else, without benefit of owners except for one trip by Nesuhi and Jay when we ended up playing five-a-side on the beach at Guaruja. Thank God Pele was away somewhere and didn't see us. Still, as the inscription says in pig-Latin on the beer tankard given as a farewell gift when I left my first job on the *Express and Echo* in Exeter, Devon, in 1958: "Nil Illegitimus Carborundum." For those of you, us, without a classical education it means: Don't Let the Bastards Grind You Down.

Between Mike Martin at one end and Krikor at the other end as the de facto GM of the Ertegun faction and the personal staffs of the high and mighty, they booked every single limousine in the State of Oregon for their use when Soccer Bowl came around in Portland. Nobody else got a look-in (though that wasn't as bad as when Ahmet drove in a chauffered Rolls from Rome to Madrid for the 1982 World Cup with another chauffered Rolls trailing behind in case the first one broke down). I just took a taxi to the game. By then I was committed to becoming President of another club. Crazy Clive was, indeed, about to rise again.

The Warner powers did call on me once, some years later, when a scandal at the Westchester Premier Theatre led to a Congressional hearing in Washington, DC. A lawyer for the Congressional committee for the occasion called me first, asking me to go down to give evidence, or else I would be subpoenaed, and who is my lawyer? I don't have one and don't need one, I replied. The next call was from a Warner lawyer, saying he would represent me, at no cost in the matter. I gave him the same reply and got back on the phone to the lawyer for Congress. I can't talk to you he said, Warner's lawyers are representing you. No, they're bloody not, I told him, I have no lawyer and I have no knowledge of what you're talking about. Well, what about Mr X and Mr Y, two of your Cosmos employees? Who? I have never heard of them, ever, and I hadn't and am glad of it, as stories and charges of racketeering and fraud and bankruptcy fraud and Mafia involvement circulated and led to indictments and conviction for some of those involved.

15

OF LEE AND UB AND HAVANA AND THE BEST TEAM I EVER COACHED

"IF YOU COME to Chicago, you'll have one big problem," said Norma Stern, "him." . . nodding towards her husband Lee, thus I had it written into my agreement that once the annual budget had been determined, I was in total control of all decisions within it. So, where's the budget from last year, I asked. Oh, we don't have one, I was told, whenever we run out of money we send down to Lee for more.

That was the measure of the Chicago chaos and Lee's genuine love of soccer and the Chicago Sting and of some of the players. Some of those players deserved Lee's affection, some (and he never spotted the difference) crept around with smiles like the Cheshire cat, talked badly of him behind his back and smirked at his generosity and friendliness. He had another side, though, volatile and, what's the word, contrary. A year after I left Chicago, of my own volition, and took over the Toronto Blizzard, we were hosts to Soccer Bowl, played between my two previous clubs, Cosmos and the Sting.

When Chicago won, as a good host and because so many of the players had been mine, I went into their locker room to congratulate them. At the entrance, Lee grabbed me by the arm and said: "I want you to know that you had nothing to do with this." Lee and I served on various League committees, too, and until Tom Werblin, one of those present at a committee meeting around that time, reminded me, I had forgotten the moment when Lee and I had a difference of opinion, heated words and eruption into combat when Lee threw a handful of ice cubes in my face and I had him pinned against the wall.

Not that Lee confined his contrariness (or his friendliness) to me; he spread both around, high and low, as he did one night after a Sting home game when he drove me home, stopping to pick up an early edition of the Chicago *Tribune* from outside their building on Michigan Avenue. A quick read convinced Lee, as we sat in his car curbside, that the *Tribune* had not done justice to the Sting that night, in either quality or quantity of coverage, so while I sat there embarrassed, Lee strode into the building and up to the sports department to remonstrate with whatever poor souls were still there preparing for later editions and hoping to go home soon. I don't think any primer on media relations has ever mentioned, as a tactic towards improvement: Storm The Sports Department Late At Night, Brandishing A Copy of the Newspaper.

Not that adventures in Chicago were confined to Lee and Michigan Avenue. For a start, there was Cuba. Cuba was interesting and not only because I could now walk down the street and buy my Cuban cigars only miles from where they were grown. Perfection. I won't talk about Cuba's politics on my theory that all politics are not only local, as Tip O'Neill once remarked, but daft.

Here is the USA, trading merrily over the years with Communist USSR, Communist China, Communist Vietnam and other forms of Ugly Dictatorships (for Communism is another word for Dictatorship) and yet refusing to do business with Communist Cuba, the smallest of the lot. Could it be the influence of those rabid anti-Castro Cubans in Miami, who were, in the main, part of the ruling class under the dictator Batista and who, in the main, let their people rot while in power? But I digress again. We were en route to play the Cuban national team in Havana as a result of efforts I had made to get the Cosmos and Pele into Cuba, part of what I viewed as an ongoing campaign to intrude soccer into people's minds by doing the newsworthy, the unexpected, like bringing the Russians and making the Cosmos the first US sports team into the People's Republic of China after Henry Kissinger's opening gambits. I had tried Cuba without response and now, in spring training 1978, we were in Barbados for training and games, thence to Haiti for games and home, when a wire arrived from the Cuban Football Association inviting us to a game.

The problem, as I saw it, was that "us" was now the Chicago Sting, not the Cosmos on whose behalf I had been making overtures. No problem, said the Cubans, we want you and now came the hard part. How do you get from Haiti to Cuba? You don't. So I chartered a plane, the only one I could find or afford; an old Dakota, last seen landing troops and supplies in Normandy in 1944 or thereabouts and off we went, propellers wheezing in the Caribbean air, shuddering from time to time, carefully picking its way through the prearranged flight path so as not to stray where Cuban anti-aircraft batteries were in wait. It got us there safely. A group of dignitaries met us at the airport, took the players in one direction and sat me down with coffee and daiquiris in the VIP lounge, most pleasant. But serious talk was afoot; I had been in Haiti for several days and before that elsewhere in the West Indies and I was without supplies. I have an important question, I said, which may affect the future of US-Cuban relations. Serious frowns and translations, yes, they said, what is it? Where, around here, can I buy a cigar, I said. (Clive Gammon was to write in a piece about me in *Sports Illustrated* some time later that the shock of my moving to the Toronto Blizzard was lessened when people realized that there I was a stroll away from an unlimited supply of Cuban cigars).

Laughs and relaxation all round and a question in return. Are you a serious cigar smoker, how many to do smoke a day? Six, I said, but I tell my wife three. At which, an exquisite robusto was produced and the rest of the visit went supremely well until, on a guided tour of Havana, I commented on some the statues of Cuban heroes in that very beautiful though, even then, deteriorating city and mentioned a statue of my home town hero Sir Francis Drake. The guides expressed disbelief and horror to know that the evil Drake was so honored. I had overlooked the fact that he had done so much damage to all things Spanish, including Cuban, in what was then known as the Spanish Main. As I said, all politics is indeed local.

Later there was Ub and I must warn you, Never carry cash to Ub. That is probably a warning which is so totally unnecessary and obscure as to be beyond consideration but I wish someone had told me. Ub, yes, it really exists, is somewhere in the Serbian hinterland, a long drive from Belgrade, a village, maybe a town, grim, grimy, gray and the home of Dragan Dzajic, at the time the captain and outstanding left winger of Yugoslavia, later voted as that country's best player of the last 50 years and a target for the Chicago Sting. We drove out there once, over roads that had seen better days, or maybe they hadn't, and did the deal. A two-year contract at reasonable terms and an upfront fee of $40,000 which, I was told, would be distributed between the player, the agent, the Yugoslav Football Association and the local, Serbian, football body. No problem, I said, I'll wire the money as soon as everything is signed. No, they said, we want it in dollars. Well, I'll wire dollars. No, they said, the Central Bank will give it to us in dinars. Ok, I said, come out with me to somewhere in the west and I'll give you dollars, cash dollars. No, they said, we'll never get them back in the country.

So, in desperation, because Djazic was really a very good player, I agreed to fly out, get Lee Stern to wire me the dollars and I would travel back—with $20,000 cash in one pocket and $20,000 cash in the other pocket. Stupid, of course, and the prospect of confinement crossed my mind as I went again through Yugoslav immigration and customs, successfully, and stayed there as we drove through forbidding, lonely country once more to Ub. Good, they said, only there's been a change. Everything stays the same except that now it is only for one year. They would not budge and neither would I. I was not paying $40,000 upfront for just one year. With the $40,000 growing heavier and more obvious by the minute, we drove back to Belgrade, though thickening fog to find the airport closed—and crowded, crowded, with hundreds of stranded travelers. So, there I was. Standing for hours, because every foot of space was filled with families and luggage and people for whom $40,000 would be the savings of several lifetimes and wishing I was anywhere else. Finally, after hours—and I do mean hours—a Lufthansa flight did arrive, I scrounged a place on it and went back out through Yugoslav customs and immigration, wondering when the heavy hand of authority would grasp my shoulder and ask what I had to declare.

When we landed in Dusseldorf and connected with a British Airways flight to London and I deposited $40,000 back into a bank, I felt so light I could have flown back to Chicago without benefit of a plane. So, never carry cash to Ub. We did sign two other Yugoslavs, as we and the whole world knew of them at the time, but there was a sign even then of the ethnic cleansing which was to come later and destroy the country. They were both represented by the same agent, a Serb, who battled for every penny for one of them, a Serb. Then we came to the other one. Oh give him $1500 a month, he said, anything will do for him, he's Muslim.

There were a number of good Yugoslav players around in the League at that time, all of them with great technical skills and many of them erratic, shall we say, in their attitude to life. Tulsa's Noel Lemon recalls: "We had some good Yugoslav players and we were playing you in Chicago and we were one up at half-time and Terry Hennessey started to talk to the team and realized one of them, one of the Yugos, was missing. So we went looking for him and finally found him outside, lying on the bench with his shirt off, sun-bathing." Not that people needed to go out into the sun to keep warm in Tulsa when Noel was there as he admits: "When it was 100 degrees in Tulsa in the summer, I used to turn off the air conditioning in the visitors' locker room. It was 150 in there. One game, we were playing Los Angeles at home, George Best was there by then, and we lost 3–0 and I was really annoyed. Went into the locker room, threw everyone out except the coach and players and really tore into them, told them you should be paying me, not me paying you, the way you play. Eugene DuChateau stood up and said he wasn't taking any more of this, so I threw a bottle of beer at the wall, hit a fan and he quickly sat down again. Well, a little while later we're playing in Edmonton and one of their writers wrote a piece about me being a fiery character and that I had once thrown a beer bottle and hit a fan. Yes, I did, but it was fan to circulate air in the locker room, not a fan in the stands. But there, I guess it made a better story." Jack Daley continues this Ode To A Lemon with his wonderful tale of an elevator ride in Seattle, to wit:

> "Shortly after the 1979 season, the Seattle Sounders ownership, despite winning the Trans-Atlantic Cup with wins over Hearts of Scotland, Southampton of England and a tie against the mighty Cosmos in New York, voted to make a coaching change. Of the various candidates interviewed, Alan Hinton, a former British winger with Wolves and Notts Forest and recently sacked by the Tulsa Roughnecks, was hired to lead the Sounders' fortune in the '80s. Hinton was eager to mold a quick striking team, one that could use the astroturf surface in the Seattle Kingdome to its advantage. He knew that Tulsa was on a tight budget and might have to release some of its better players. After giving me a run down of the players he wanted, I started working a trade with Noel Lemon. Noel confessed that he had to pare down his player payroll to

meet his club's budget guidelines. He was willing to trade striker Roger Davies, midfielder Roy Graves, defender David Nish and the rights to Canadian goalkeeper Jack Brand. Brand was especially appealing to us since he could play a key position and fill one of the required North American player slots. In return, I agreed to send striker Tommy Ord, defender Bruce Rudroff and an undisclosed amount of cash to Tulsa for the three British players and the option on Brand. The four new Sounders turned Seattle's ship around. After losing its second game of the season, Seattle reeled off 13 consecutive wins to lead the Western Conference.

"On Tulsa's first visit to Seattle in that 1980 season, Lemon accompanied his team to the game. I met Noel and escorted him up the elevator to the visiting team box. On the ride up, I introduced him to Cale Campbell, a Viet Nam veteran and the elevator operator who met every guest with a huge smile and a warm greeting. I mentioned to Cale, who lost his right arm up to his elbow in the war, that Mr. Lemon was the Tulsa general manager, and the person who provided us with the four former Roughneck players. The game was particularly one-sided. The Sounders won 6–1, Davies had two goals and Graves, Nish and Brand had stellar performances. Immediately after the final whistle, I headed for the press elevator to descend to the players' locker room. At the elevator door, I ran into Noel and needless to say, he wasn't a happy Irishman. In fact, I think he was scowling. "Sorry," I said, "we just had a lucky night." We both got on the elevator, packed with the soccer writers also heading for the players' area. On the way down, operator Campbell announced to everyone on board, that "Noel Lemon, general manager of the Roughnecks was present, and all Seattle thanks him for sending us Davies, Graves, Nish and Brand." As the elevator reached the ground level, Campbell asked Noel rather pointedly, "Who are you going to send us next season, Mr. Lemon?" The doors slid open. As Lemon walked out and without turning around, he bellowed, "a new elevator operator!" Yes, Noel recalled . . . it was banner night there and all over the place they had these banners "Thank You Noel Lemon."

While we're on the subject, we should not let it be thought that Noel's antics, or admissions, ended there. "We were playing at Dallas early in the season and they were coming back to Tulsa a few weeks later. With a couple of minutes to go their center-half Steve Petcher kicked Billy Caskey and Caskey nutted him and was sent off. As they were leaving the field, I said to Petcher—go on, then, why don't you pick on me, come on—and we got into a bit of a scrap and people came round, Glen Myernick was one, and separated us. When we got into the locker room, Bill Foulkes (Tulsa coach and once of the great Manchester United team of Sir Matt Busby) said:" What on earth are you doing, Noel?" I said, wait until you see the papers in the next couple of weeks, that'll get 'em going for the return game. And we doubled our attendance when Dallas came—16,000 instead of 8,000.

"Ward Lay had moved Team Hawaii to Tulsa in 1978 and I traded away the entire team except for one player, Charlie Mitchell. We played our first game on April Fool's Day, my sister-in-law passed away that day and one of our players, Milan Davidan, broke his leg and never played again. Ward sold equity in the club to local people and one of them was Carl Moore, who had a full-sized field built at his home and hired Davidan to coach his son—Joe-Max Moore. He turned into a pretty fair player, didn't he—US World Cup team, English Premier Division? Nicest lad you could ever wish to meet. Joe-Max and my son Noel Jr. were ball boys and I can't count the number of times I had to go down and threaten them because instead of standing each side of the goal and paying attention, they were way behind the goal kicking the ball about." That reminded my own son Robert of one incident when he was a Cosmos ball boy: "I threw the ball back in quickly and one of the Cosmos players, Mark Liveric I think it was, thought the ball was still in play and ran in and scored a goal. What a fuss there was when it was disallowed, arguing and shouting. I stood there feeling guilty about the whole thing with people giving me dirty looks. Nothing as bad mind you as when Shep Messing was really upset with me one day when he said I kicked the ball to him too hard. I must have been about six at the time!"

Which reminds me of the best team I ever coached, in fact the only team I ever coached until resuming my youth coaching career at the ridiculous age of 73. The Heathcote Hornets they were called and it was the best time I ever had on the playing field, taking this bunch of 6- and 7-year-olds and coaching this same active little mob, with very few changes, all the way until they disappeared into high school. We won the Scarsdale

League every year, finished second in the Westchester County League and won the KLM Westchester Youth Cup, which was for all-star teams, with the same boys who played week in, week out. Along the way to that major Cup Final, at Mount Vernon's Memorial Stadium against Brewster, with flags and national anthem and several hundred people in the stands, we beat a team from New Rochelle 2–1, a team coached by Chuck Blazer, later a founder with me of the American Professional Soccer League in the dead days after the NASL and later still General Secretary of CON-CACAF and a member of the FIFA Executive Committee. Maybe so, but we still beat them. But the nicest thing was a letter in the local Scarsdale *Inquirer* headed:

> Here's to Coach Toye. Clive Toye has been more than just our sons' soccer coach for the past five years. These boys are truly lucky to have had the opportunity to work with him. The skills and sportsmanship learned under his leadership will never be lost. Each boy was always treated with dignity and played fairly.
>
> Clive Toye is a credit to Heathcote and we all thank him for contributing so importantly to the development of our children during their formative years.
>
> Thank you, Clive.
>
> HEATHCOTE HORNETS and PARENTS

What could be more rewarding than that? Not much, though about 30 years after they had kicked their first ball, I did get a slew of e-mails from a number of them at the time of my induction into the Hall of Fame. From one: Thanks for everything. The Hornets was one of the best experiences in my life. From a scrofulous little swine (one of my more affectionate names for them, by the way) who still plays soccer. From another: I can remember it as if it were yesterday, all of the practices and games. Pig in the middle is one of my kids' drills and "if in doubt, kick it out." I have never had them practice with no shoes at 6 am when the grass is cold and wet but I do remember how you would tell us you would do it to keep the sense of touch sharp. What you taught us out there on the field on those simple mornings about teamwork, about coaching, about leadership couldn't be taught in a classroom. And yet it lives on, not only in that bunch of 4th graders frozen in time at the Supply Field but in who we all became and what we now impart to our own kids. From yet another: Your motivational words to us in 7th grade "you're playing like a bunch of bloody fairies on a Christmas tree" still makes me howl. Did you use the same line with Pele. And more. From the Head of Doctoral Studies at a prestigious university, from corporate executives, from partners in distinguished law firms (well, I didn't know the little buggers would turn into lawyers, did I?)

What I do know, is that once upon a time I could hold my own against as many as five or six of them. Now I am happy if, in a one-on-one game with my grandson, I can hold the score to a respectable 10–1, even 10–2 on occasion. It is a chastening thought. The Hornets remained the only New York team for whom I wished only success and happiness, naturally, but a quirk of the schedule kept the Sting and the Cosmos apart in 1978, my first year away, but we played them in 1979 in Chicago. May 10 it was. We whacked them 3–0. Even better though was Toronto's later 4–1 win at Giants Stadium, ho ho ho, I really remember that one, in 1982, and in 1984 the last ever meeting of the club I had once built and the club I had now built was another good moment, 4–0 to us. Of course, we had lost a few to them along the way, but I am ignoring those, after all this is my book.

The search for players for the Sting continued, of course, although the search was not always a distant one. One day the receptionist phoned in to say there was a visitor in the office—"guy here from Holland" I was told "he wants a tryout." My first thought was to send him, politely on his way, because we were past the days of giving tryouts to any itinerant and out-of-work player. But courtesy won over, I asked him in, saw the clubs he had played for and gave him the tryout he asked for. Then immediately signed this very good, very busy, very professional midfield player who much later became one of the best-known managers in the world, including that of Holland and Glasgow Rangers. That was Dick Advocaat, that was. Doubtful if better players just walked in anyone's door. Not so simple was the signing of Tomas Sjoberg, the blond bearded Viking who did so well up front for Sweden in the 1978 World Cup in Argentina, and had two choices in 1979 when a lucrative contract in Saudi Arabia ran out. He could go home in the spring, enjoy a magnificent Swedish summer . . . and pay about 90% of his Saudi income in Swedish taxes, to support the all-embracing socialism of his native land. Or, he could lounge on a beach somewhere until the tax year passed and go home in the fall. I was driving onto the car ferry from Copenhagen to Malmo in southern Sweden, Skona, with my friend Borje Lantz when I heard about it and decided to give Tomas a different option—play for the Chicago Sting, keep fit, see America and earn some more money; keeping all of it from the Swedish tax man.

Now, if you have never tried to back out from a car ferry with a line of cars sitting, hooting right behind you, I advise you not to try. But back out we did, right back to Kastrup airport and on the phone to Tomas, in Saudi Arabia somewhere. It took a while but it all worked out in the end and he had a great season for us. In the end, I think I knew the tax codes of a dozen nations; it made a great deal of difference to players who wanted to know what would end up in their pockets, especially if the tax authorities of two nations wanted their pound, or rather dollar, of flesh. It was neither the first nor the last time that Borje Lantz, friend, club director, promoter, entrepreneur, fluent in six languages and able to communicate in six others and wise in the ways of the world, helped me achieve something. He even taught me Swedish. I can say Femty Fem, with the best of them, and that's it. Well, you try learning Swedish. (It means 55 by the way, to save you looking it up and I learned that because it sounded funny. Period.)

On this occasion, Borje helped me and made Gordon Jago, by then coach at Tampa Bay Rowdies, absolutely furious with the both of us. He thought he had Sjoberg wrapped up and was sitting in Florida, waiting for it to gently fall into place. In the meantime, we were exchanging oaths in several languages and even more dialects as we backed off the car ferry through the lines of traffic and frantically shoved Kroner into a phone at Kastrup to keep open the connection to Saudi Arabia. Borje lived mostly in Cascais, that lovely little place outside Lisbon, where one of his neighbors was his fellow Swede, Sven Goran Eriksson, coach of Benfica at the time, and coach of IFK Gothenberg, Lazio and England at other times. When the US was looking for a coach to take the team in the 1994 World Cup, I recommended Svennis as well as Arsene Wenger and Gerard Houllier as the best men for the US job. The then general secretary Hank Steinbrecher did get as far as meeting Svennis but the impression I got was that they were all too full of character and professional ability to allow Hank, or his boss Alan Rothenberg, to feel comfortable. The last time Alan ever asked my opinion was one day in the St. Regis Hotel in Manhattan when he raised the name of Bora Milutinovic as a potential national team coach. As I was saying: "I wouldn't touch him with a barge pole," I could see from Alan's face that that was not the answer he was looking for. He wanted confirmation of a choice already made, not an opinion. Well, that is certainly one way of stopping people from asking your opinion about anything,

16

ON 'THE BOYS, THE BOYS' PLUS A FEW OLD MEN

BAFANA, BAFANA. The Boys. The Boys. You hear that expression a lot these days, in the years since the end of apartheid in South Africa and that country's reentry into world sport, especially rugby, cricket and, of course, football, the sport of the black majority. That's what they call their national team as they go out to do battle where once they were forbidden. But I don't think so much of The Boys, The Boys who are playing freely and earning mightily at home, overseas and in the World Cup. I think of the Old Men, the Old Men whom apartheid, and a white reluctance to look at black players, stopped them from becoming the world figures they should have become.

I knew three, though there were others whom the crowds worshipped in Orlando Stadium, in Soweto, in Attridgeville, in Alexandra. First, there was Kaizer Motaung, center forward for the Atlanta Chiefs. When Kaizer went home, he took the Atlanta logo, changed the colors from red and blue to yellow and black and formed his own club, Kaizer Chiefs, today the most popular pro club in South Africa. Then there was Ephraim Jomo Sono, whom I signed first for the Cosmos and then again later, after he had had a rough time in Colorado and Atlanta, for the Toronto Blizzard. What a brilliant, electric player was Jomo; so good that Juventus was ready to pay $750,000 for him and make him the first black African player in Italy's Serie A and with its most prestigious club, to boot. Juventus President Giampiero Boniperti was in the crowd there, that day in Toronto's CNE Stadium, when we played Tulsa and the contracts were ready to sign and Jomo fractured an ankle, four minutes before half time. Prone to put on weight, Jomo spent the winter doing just that and never came back to his best. So he went home, too, to form Jomo Cosmos and play in South Africa's top league in competition with Kaizer's Chiefs and, still as Chairman of the Jomo Cosmos, to become South Africa's coach in the World Cup of 2002.

The third one was Patrick Pule Ace Ntsolengoe, a quiet, gentle Tswana whose only complaint during the time I knew him was when the South African government took away his South African passport and declared him a citizen of the mock country of Bophutatswana, one of the homelands the Afrikaaner government created. We, and he, had to go through contortions, then, to get him a travel document from a country which no one other than South Africa recognized and get into Canada and over the border into the USA for games. It wasn't easy but it was child's play compared to what came next. Ace's agent Albertus "Toy" Mostert phoned frantically one day just before spring training to say Ace was in jail outside Johannesburg at a tough, rural and mining place called Randfontein, the township (the name given to all the black shanty towns close by white cities) for Krugersdorp. He had been caught driving a stolen car; stolen and given to him by one of the group of Tsotses, criminal gangs, who worshipped Ace.

So, off I went to Johannesburg and Krugersdorp and the Chief of Police, a man with a bull-neck, sun-hardened skin, a typical Afrikaaner name, like van der Merwe or some such and the nickname of Cowboy. I explained my purpose. Why do you want this bleddy bleck, man, he said. We've got millions of them, take as many as you like. We hired a lawyer and I sang a few choruses of Sarie Marais in one of the local police bars that night which is probably what did it because I don't think any Afrikaaner had ever heard a rooinek (a redneck, an Englishman) sing Sarie Marais in Afrikaans, bad Afrikaans, before. Sarie Marais is like *America, the Beautiful* to an American, *Waltzing Matilda* to an Aussie or *Land of Hope and Glory* to the British; not the official anthem but a song of the heart. Never did let on where I learned it, which was in Korea in the Commonwealth Division, where we had Aussies and Kiwis and Canucks and Ghurkas and a few South Africans. So, sometimes, when there was a break in the action, as they say, and the beer ration came up, we would have a sing-song and learn from the others. If you ever go to Nepal and hear an aged Ghurka singing *Glorious Devon,* don't be surprised.

Ace, too, formed his own club, Ace Kicks, in memory of the first NASL club where he was lionized, Minnesota Kicks. All three of them could have played in top European football; probably alongside others whom I saw less frequently like Ace Mnini, Teenage Dladla, Webster Lichaba, Lucas "Masterpieces" Moripe, who arrived in the NASL too late in his life and too alone in a dramatically different culture, and the whites like Neil Roberts and the three Wegerles, Steve, Roy and Jeff, who played alongside their black countrymen in the NASL and in the only desegregated part of South Africa at the time—soccer. We went on a preseason tour of Italy in 1984 playing the likes of Juventus, Internazionale and Sampdoria. Ace was the best player on the field. So it was a particular pleasure that Ace was inducted into the US Soccer Hall of Fame in 2003, at the same time as me. I remembered him; so, too, I am glad to say, did everyone else. As a sad postscript, the very day I was doing the final review of this book, I received the news that Ace had been found dead in his car in Johannesburg. RIP, Ace.

Let us now look at another set of Old Men, the Old Men who, it was widely reported and believed, made up the entire rosters of NASL teams, Old Men with slowing mind and thickening sinews who could not get a job elsewhere in the wide world of football. Well, for a moment let us forget Pele, courted at the same time by Real Madrid and Juventus, and Franz, who went back to play for Hamburg in the Bundesliga when his four-year Cosmos contract was over, or Roberto Bettega, who played in the European Cup Final against Hamburg in Athens one night and signed for Toronto the next day or Tomas Sjoberg, waylaid on the way home to Sweden to continue his career in the national team and the likes of Jimmy Nicholl, back home to play for Northern Ireland and then later for Glasgow Rangers. And those are just my players; others club had similar "current" players. More striking is the catalogue of young nobodies who played in the NASL and went on, home, to great things. Thanks to the eagle eye of Joe Mallett, ex-Birmingham boss who was our scout and assistant coach, we signed Steve Hunt from Aston Villa reserves for $17,000. He went back for twenty times that much to West Bromwich Albion and a future career for England. Then there was this kid from Carlisle, Peter Beardsley, whom Tony Waiters, once an England player himself, took out to Vancouver and turned into a man who won a trunk-

load of England caps and a magnificent career with Liverpool and Newcastle United.

Bruce Grobelaar, from nowhere, left Vancouver to become a fixture in
goal in many of Liverpool's great years, 19-year-old Graham Sounness
played with Montreal, a young lad called Trevor Francis was at Detroit, as
was Mark Hately; the first went on to be a star for Scotland, the last two to
star for England. Hugo Sanchez became one of Real Madrid's greatest
stars and leading goalscorer after his time at San Diego and the Cosmos
Paraguayan pair, Robert Cabanas and Julio Cesar Romero, Romerito,
went on to outstanding years in Brazilian football. That is not even touching on the loan players who came over under a formal agreement with the
Football League. It cost us nothing in transfer fees, it saved the English
clubs the players' summer wages and it meant a large inflow of current
First Division players; yes, current players, who then went back to continue being current, yes current, First Division players.

Noel Lemon recalls that one day, Tulsa fielded an entire starting line
up of national team players.

> "One night we had a get-together at the house after Jimmy Nicholl came
> down with Toronto. We had Jimmy Nick, Billy Caskey, Victor More-
> land, Chris McGrath and David McCreery, five of them Northern Ireland
> internationals, plus Edvilsson, the Icelander we had just bought from
> Celtic and Dainafard, the Iranian, straight from the 1982 World Cup . . .
> about 14 international players in the room that night. And don't forget
> the 1982 World Cup and Northern Ireland beating Spain. Along with all
> the players identified as being with clubs like Tottenham Hotspur and
> Manchester United in the Ireland lineup were David McCreery (Tulsa)
> and Jimmy Nicholl (Toronto)."

Like most of us, Noel concedes there were some bad signings:

> "A couple who bad injuries were pretty well known, I thought. Al
> Miller signed one of them, for Dallas, Klaus Topmuller. He said that
> Topmuller would be better than Chinaglia. I said if he had two legs he'd
> have half a chance. Then there was the preacher man, Peter Warner,
> who was suddenly running everything in Portland. He signed Robbie
> Rensenbrink, who'd been a great player, even though he hit the post
> instead of scoring to win the World Cup for Holland in 1978, against
> Argentina, but he had a bad injury. So I'm standing next to the preach-

er, at the bottom of the ramp at Portland, behind the goal, before the game has even started and down the ramp comes this ambulance, lights flashing, horn going, and he says "who's that for?" and I said Robbie Rensenbrink. He glared daggers at me. He's the one who spent half a million on buying a center half from Coventry, Gary Collier. Not a bad player but half a million for a defender no one in Portland had ever heard of?"

Out in anglophile Seattle in the late 70s, Jimmy Gabriel and then Alan Hinton could put almost an entire team of First Division players from England on the field; one of them, Harry Redknapp, spent three years with the Sounders. Milan Mandaric was owner of the San Jose Earthquakes then. A quarter century later they linked up to take Portsmouth into the English Premiership. Were some NASL players past their best? Yes. Were some as good as they ever were? Yes. Were some still at the dawn of successful careers at the highest levels in the world? Yes. As I said earlier in another context, the truth's the truth.

One more truth is that I forgot the lessons of Baltimore, 1967. At the end my first season in Toronto, I wanted to change coaches and let Keith Eddy go. Keith from Sheffield United and Watford, via a spell as captain and central defender for the Cosmos, was not what I wanted and so the decision was made except . . . except . . . he, like Doug Millward's son in 1967 Baltimore, was ill and in a hospital and, though not life threatening, really bad. And, as the saying goes, I bottled it and did not fire him and so we went on into 1981 with things going from bad to worse and relationships strained to the max and the whole thing keeping back the Blizzard's revival for a full year. So bad did it get that Keith left of his own accord in mid-season, with nastiness and recriminations all round, and it wasn't until that off-season that Bob Houghton, once of Malmo FF in the European Cup Final against Nottingham Forest, and later national coach of China, later still of Uzbekistan and India, was hired and we began to make progress. As I said to myself in Baltimore, if you know you have to do something unpleasant, do it now. It can only get worse.

(There must, incidentally, be something in the water or in the genes in Canada, a massive country which often threatens to break apart. The Blizzard uniform, in predominantly Anglo-Saxon Ontario, where so many loyalists settled after the Revolutionary War was predominantly red, the red of the redcoats of old. When le Manic de Montreal came into the league in 1981, they chose an emblem of the French fleur de lys and the pale blue color worn by French soldiers as they and their Iriquois allies flitted through the New England forests to massacre settlers.)

Once we became organized, the results and the crowds started coming but the most pleasant and surprising arrival of all was dated April 22, 1982 with a handwritten note Dear Clive, Delighted results are going well for you. Keep it up. Best wishes, Stan Matthews.

Sir Stanley, greatest of the players in the immediate post-war period, was then living, on and off, in Burlington, Ontario but I had no idea he was paying attention to us but I used to collect autographs and that is one I definitely kept. Sir Stan still played soccer, even into his 60s, when retired on Malta and turning out for the local Post Office team. "Oh, I could still go past them," he said "but when they knocked me down it took a lot longer to get up." I know what it's like, Stan, every time I play against my grandson.

While that was a pleasant surprise, I'm still not sure about another—planned and carried out by Dale Barnes, noted Canadian TV sportscaster, with a 3-hour high-rated Saturday show. As Dale told with glee:

> "Early in the show I announced that the Blizzard were dead and kept the story going throughout the show, with quotes from people all over town, the Canadian Soccer Association, players, civic people, saying how sad it was and what a shame. There were people in the studio, real Blizzard fans, crying about it. Then at the end of the show, I told them it was all a pack of lies but just think, if we lose the Blizzard, this is how it will be; the end of soccer in Toronto. Bruce Wilson wanted to punch me because his wife heard it and was so upset. But your attendance was way up for the next game. The papers were full of the story next day. One of them compared it to the shock of that Orson Welles' broadcast about the War of the Worlds, back in the 30s."

Toronto's last owner Karsten von Wersebe asked a question once when we were interviewing a general manager candidate, Tommy Scallen: "With whom do you relate best? Those you work for or those who work for you? I had never heard that very penetrating question before. I forget how Tommy answered but by the time you finish this book you ought to be able to guess what mine would have been. Requests I am happy to fulfill; orders do not sit well. Generally speaking I have followed my wife's orders for nearly 50 years and I suppose I must have followed orders in the Army, though not many. The military asks a lot of its young men and, at the age of 19, for many months, for many hours at a time, I was basically in charge of all signals for an infantry brigade, in combat in Korea, and the only one in the brigade who was security cleared to handle top secret traffic. This top secret stuff was sometimes droll and sometimes desperate, ranging from the General letting the Brigadier know he was popping in for tea to the other extreme of US 7th Marines, under attack by two Chinese divisions on a hill known as The Hook, asking if any British help was available. There was—and a couple of days before my 20th birthday, we went over with the Black Watch to hold the hill. As the French would say "plus ca change, plus ce meme chose" (the more things change, the more they stay the same); in the spring of 2003, the 7th Marines and the 1st Black Watch were side by side again in Iraq. Though, of course, the French weren't anywhere to be found, neither in Korea nor in Iraq.

17

THANK YOU, MONTY PYTHON

THIS IS THE tale of The Parrot Burial Kit, PollyUrineX, Monty Python and how to make sure the Canadian national anthem gets booed. In Canada. Quite simple, really. You take the NASL quarter finals between the Toronto Blizzard and the Vancouver Whitecaps, one of the truly fine clubs of the NASL in one of the world's truly fine cities, understanding that Eastern Canada and Western Canada don't like each other very much, for a start. Then you take the Whitecaps utter determination to reach Soccer Bowl '83 because the beautiful BC Stadium was newly built, the Whitecaps were going to play there and Soccer Bowl '83 was to be held there, too, and what could be more perfect than to play in the Soccer Bowl in your own, new, stadium filled with your own fans?

Then you take their goalkeeper Tino Lettieri, who had a stuffed toy parrot as a mascot which he carried onto the field and placed in the back of the nets and wasn't a bad `keeper, if prone to emotion and volatility i.e. he could be upset. It was a best-of-three series and we lost the first leg in British Columbia. For the second leg in Toronto's CNE Stadium, I thought I would see how upset Lettieri could become. He had raised my ire, which never did need much raising when a game was at stake, by picking up his parrot from the back of the net and using it to knock the ball into place for a goal kick. So Tino and his parrot were fair game as far as I was concerned and far is where I was prepared to go. Some of the media warmed to the "Let's See Tino Twitch" campaign we were murmuring about and Dale Barnes even went so far as to tell his audience to take buckets of water to the game to drown Tino's pet (stuffed, I remind you) parrot. We (well I, to be honest, because late in life I have realized that what I really wanted to be was a Monty Python script writer), took it a bit further on game day. First, I ordered the Whitecaps mascot, who was a human parrot designed to support and enlarge the Tino theme, to be banned from the field. Then had a big sign posted in their locker room: 'Warning. This Room Has Been Sprayed With PollyUrineX. Dangerous To Your Health.' Next, as Tino ran towards his goal, two men, dressed in black, with black hats and plumes, carried a small shovel and a small box and placed them by the goal. The label said: Parrot Burial Kit.

How much those pranks helped us win the second leg is questionable but they certainly helped when we flew again to Vancouver for the third and deciding game, sending Tino a stack of sympathy cards on the death of his parrot in advance. Tense and hostile are fair descriptions of the atmosphere when we got there, with two sets of airline tickets in hand— one to go home, if beaten, and one to go on to San Jose for the first semi- final game just two days hence. So with a filled stadium and angry crowd above our heads, with a rude welcome to be had, we then had the team talk to end all team talks, a video of the Monty Python Dead Parrot sketch, followed by the Monty Python Mounties' sketch. The Dead Parrot sketch, for those who never saw it (and a chance to laugh again for those who did) ends with John Cleese describing the parrot he has bought from the furtive shop-keeper Michael Palin, who insists that the parrot, a Nor- wegian Blue, for heaven's sake, is resting or stunned: Says the increasing- ly indignant Cleese:

> 'E's not pinin'! 'E's passed on! This parrot is no more! He has ceased to be! 'E's expired and gone to meet 'is maker! 'E's a stiff! Bereft of life, 'e rests in peace! If you hadn't nailed 'im to the perch 'e'd be pushing up the daisies! 'Is metabolic processes are now 'istory! 'E's off the twig! 'E's kicked the bucket, 'e's shuffled off 'is mortal coil, rundown the cur- tain and joined the bleedin' choir invisibile!! THIS IS AN EX-PAR- ROT!!

With laughter mounting in the locker room, we then went on to the spliced-in Mounties' sketch that begins with bluff, outdoor men in Moun- ties's red coats singing heartily in chorus to a soloist and then turning into Python absurdity:

> **SOLO:** I'm a lumberjack, and I'm okay. I sleep all night and I work all day.
> **MOUNTIES:** He's a lumberjack, and he's okay. He sleeps all night and he works all day.

SOLO: I cut down trees. I eat my lunch. I go to the lavatory. On Wednesdays I go shoppin' And have buttered scones for tea.

MOUNTIES: He cuts down trees. He eats his lunch. He goes to the lavatory. On Wednesdays he goes shoppin' And has buttered scones for tea. He's a lumberjack, and he's okay. He sleeps all night and he works all day.

SOLO: I cut down trees. I skip and jump. I like to press wild flowers. I put on women's clothing And hang around in bars.

MOUNTIES: He cuts down trees. He skips and jumps. He likes to press wild flowers. He puts on women's clothing And hangs around in bars?! He's a lumberjack, and he's okay. He sleeps all night and he works all day.

SOLO: I cut down trees. I wear high heels, Suspendies, and a bra. I wish I'd been a girlie, Just like my dear Papa.

MOUNTIES: He cuts down trees. He wears high heels, Suspendies, and a bra?! [talking] What's this? Wants to be a girlie?! Oh, My! And I thought you were so rugged! Poofter! [singing] He's a lumberjack, and he's okay. He sleeps all night and he works all day.

My lasting memory of our locker room just before the players had to line up in the tunnel is of Neil Roberts, our center-forward, a tall, angular South African, kneeling, bent over with the head touching the floor, rocking with laughter. The tension was gone, evaporated at those loony Pythons and the Dead Parrot. Neil Roberts scored our winning goal with a shot which went in off the shins of Tino Lettieri. Vancouver was not pleased.

Two days later, we were in San Jose for the semifinal first game and the perfect example of where stubborn, out-of-touch ownership ran rampant. Carl Berg, who may have known it all except anything about the game he had now bought into, had replaced Milan Mandaric as the owner and Milan, of course, was a died-in-the wool soccer fan, originally from Serbia. So, there we are, with a big and passionate San Jose Earthquakes crowd, baying for blood, and our lads just 48 hours out of the maelstrom of Vancouver and we manage to hold them 0–0 and the game goes to the shootout phase. With the last kick to be taken, we need to score to win the game and the crowd is so into it, so loud, so wonderfully alive that David Byrne, the taker, can not hear the referee's whistle to start his shootout attempt. At least, being David Byrne and cocky as they come, he might have pretended just to psyche out the goalkeeper, but eventually he takes it, scores and we win. Now, I can understand the gloom and disappointment that comes with defeat; I've experienced it enough times, but it was still a great soccer occasion, with both teams running their legs off and the crowd passionate, passionate, passionate. Do you think Carl Berg got it, do you think he understood underneath his disappointment, that the crowd had not let up for 90 minutes, plus time for the deciding moments? That this is what sport is about? No, all he could say, brusquely, rudely, that it was a lousy 0–0 game, that we had played defensively and this was ruining the whole game. There's none so blind as those who refuse to see. Anyway, just to make up for it, we whacked them 2–0 in the second game in Toronto and that was that. On to Soccer Bowl, back to Vancouver.

But if getting to Soccer Bowl '83 had been fun, being there was not. It wasn't the booing of the 62,000 crowd that made it unpleasant, even when they booed their own national anthem, nor the booing from the black tie crowd at the Soccer Bowl Week banquet. No, it was stupidity far from the stadium that made it a difficult time. First, there was Howard Samuels, President of the League and successor to Woosnam, an amiable enough man with as little interest in or feeling for football as I have for climbing nude up Mount Everest. League rules had caught up with Tulsa Roughnecks striker Ron Futcher and, for being a bad boy, he was suspended for Soccer Bowl. Enter the Roughnecks owners to tell Samuels that if Futcher was not allowed to play, they would not turn up for the game and 62,000 people and national TV would have a half-empty playing field to look at. Howard asked me if we would play in any event and thinking more about the disgrace to soccer than myself, or my club, I said we would play anybody, anytime, anywhere. So Howard allowed Futcher to play and he scored one of the goals in our totally unexpected defeat.

But that was not the end of the things that should not have been. We did not lose just because Futcher was allowed to play. We lost because we did not play well and two players who were grossly off form were David Byrne, normally buzzing around up front, nonstop, and Jimmy Nicholl, our midfield dynamo. The buzz from Byrne, son of the great West Ham and England forward Johnny Byrne, was absent. The dynamo of Nicholl, bought from Manchester United, where he was a regular for United and

Northern Ireland, was flat. It was weeks later that we found out the pair of them were seen leaving a local nightspot in the early hours of the morning of Soccer Bowl. So if Samuels' choice of action was wrong, what does that make theirs?

We had to get over that defeat fast, so I went to the office right from the red-eye from Vancouver and typed up a note (yes, Virginia, we still had typewriters then): THE 1984 SEASON BEGINS AT 9.30 A.M TOMORROW. SEASON TICKETS WILL BE ON SALE SHORTLY. PRE-SEASON TRAINING WILL BEGIN IN MID-MARCH IN ORLANDO FLORIDA. And so it did. All in all, though, not a bad season, good results for us, better acceptance by the public, better crowds and along the way the chance to learn a few lessons about people. There was Blizzard board member Johnny Lombardi, nice old chap, important radio network owner, awarded the Order of Canada. When I was young, he told me, there used to be signs at the swimming pools. No dogs or Italians. There was Dr. Henry Kissinger, by now the Chairman of the NASL and a great, gravelly speaker of many things worldly and vital. He liked soccer, for sure, but had less than a full repertoire of wisdom and insights about the game. Thus one tale was oft-told, and no worse for its repetition. "At Furth, in Germany, as a young man I played in many exciting and very high scoring games, he would say." Pause. "I was the goalkeeper." There was Karsten von Wersebe, new owner of the club, with his solitary remark about our season; the one and only. It was just after the defeat in Soccer Bowl when he said it: "We must do better next time." Period. I did not relay it to the team. There was Giampiero Boniperti, former great player, then coach, then President of Juventus and by now also a member of our board. "Tell me now," he asked, "what did you really pay Pele?" I told him. "Well," he said, "that's about what we would have paid him at the time."

There was the aforementioned Howard Samuels, too, President of the League who was never quite sure who he was or where he was. At the Soccer Bowl banquet in Vancouver, British Colombia, Canada, he said: Welcome to Vancouver, Washington. At Toronto's airport, arriving and seeing lines of people leaning over the barricades waiting to meet people, Howard—once a candidate for Governor of New York State—walked along them all, shaking hands and thanking them for coming. At a reception full of Canadian soccer and political dignitaries, on the dizzy heights of Toronto's CNE Tower, Howard ended a stirring speech on the future of soccer by saying: "And one day the United States will win the World Cup." He was surprised at the lack of enthusiasm in the audience. Ted Howard reminded me that at the press conference in Vancouver, he introduced Pele as Pepe and you'll have to work out for yourself what he did to Ron Futcher's name.

Then there was the question I asked myself: Why, oh why was I able to get Bobby-gol (the nickname of the famous Juventus and Italy's World Cup striker Robert Bettega) on a free transfer from Juventus? He still had a couple of years at the top to go, so it wasn't that. Juventus President Giampiero Boniperti was a very nice man, even joined the Blizzard Board, but that didn't pay more than enough for a couple of good meals, so it wasn't that. I found out when I learned that Bobby-gol was also Bobby-ambitious, having private meetings with the owner, Karsten von Wersebe, and having conversations unlikely to have been about the weather. Possibly, I asked myself, Boniperti, who, himself, had risen from the ranks of the great Juventus team of the 50s, alongside John Charles and Omar Sivori, to become coach and then President, preferred Bobby-gol to seek his future in Toronto rather than Torino. Who might be more easily replaced? Well, the Blizzard were dead before too long and guess who became Vice President and the man in charge of Juventus. Roberto Bettega.

But if there was silliness and stupidity following the Blizzard in 1983, there was greater nonsense happening elsewhere. After all, our silliness and the compounded stupidity in Vancouver only cost someone a game. What was happening elsewhere was costing us some of our diminishing shreds of respect, more of our remaining hopes for life eternal. Team America was the last fling, the last wild throw to find an answer to something; anything. In itself, not a bad idea. We wanted, needed, to start preparing a US national team for the better days to come and here they could play together all season, with a home in the nation's capital, and American prowess on the line. But even good ideas need time to develop (which, thinking back, is probably as good an epitaph for the NASL as any) and this good idea was rushed into being in no time at all. One of Howard Samuels' friends, Robert Lifton, was given the franchise and it was a disaster. Some clubs, among them Cosmos (surprise, surprise) refused to let their US players go to Team America, so Rick Davis and Steve Moyers, for example, never got there and Team America finished with the worst record in the league: most losses (20), fewest goals (33), fewest points (79, compared to the Cosmos 194). They also equaled the shortest life span of any franchise in the league: one year. Ted Howard experienced one more of Howard's verbal problems: "We were on the way to a Team America event and Bob Lifton said, remember Howard, no names, just hello, no names."

Lucky for Howard he had only 12 team names to remember in 1983 and even fewer to come as three more went the way of all flesh before the coming season. That farsighted man Sonny Werblin called them Little Bangs, the signs of troubled times to come, and now they were too loud for anyone to ignore; even when being booed by 62,000 people in Vancouver.

18

BIG BANG, LITTLE BANG, SILENCE

EVERY TERMINAL ILLNESS must begin somewhere in the body when there's a spring in the step, a bloom on the cheek and mortality is for someone else. So it was with us. With a future of glory still being propounded, and even existing in many places, the annual check-up with the family doctor would have had him reaching for the prescription pad and issuing dire warnings to lead a cleaner life.

Our annual check-ups, or annual general meetings, had too many patients bent on self destruction who threw away the prescription as they left the room, if they bothered to pick it up at all. Hence, this long good-bye that began when all seemed bright and Giants Stadium was packing 'em in. Ted Howard, long-time league administrator, speaks solemnly still of one of those days: "I flew over the stadium in the Warner helicopter the night of the first sell-out, 77,691 if I remember it correctly. It was a heart-stopping sight." That same year, 1977, we spent an entire year, of one week-end a month, to work on the Long Term Strategic Plan, which at the end said, among many other things: We have 18 clubs. Six are doing well. Six are okay and can be improved. Six either have to be moved to better markets or taken over by new owners or dumped.

Lamar Hunt was part of that Long Term group, so were Lee Stern and Jim Ruben of Minnesota and Steve Danzansky from DC and myself. As Lee Stern put it: "So many week ends. We put together a great package and Phil never paid any attention to it. He just never paid any attention to it. We talked about not expanding and Phil was always wanting to expand to get more revenue from the sale of expansion teams. The other thing was to concentrate on regional television, not on national television. Nobody cared whether Tulsa played Fort Lauderdale."

Thus outside that committee, Phil Woosnam was working on new franchises, at $3 million a pop, and when it came to a vote at the annual meeting, the idea of six new clubs coming in, with $18 million to be divided, was too strong a lure. I am sure it was not an easy sell but the Cosmos crowds, the glitterati, the attention paid by the media (the New York *Daily News* had these vast posters on their delivery vans: **We Cover the Cosmos** with a huge figure of a soccer player), the term Cosmos Country cropping up everywhere, go to Giants Stadium, feel the buzz, see Mick Jagger or lord knows who sitting a few seats away and, if you've got the money, it could be irresistible. Who was right, Phil and those who voted for expansion? Or those of us in the antiexpansion, antinational TV group? Well, we know that those who won the vote and the battle lost the war, for sure; we'll never know whether the other road would also have led to eventual failure. That's an answer as difficult to find as the resting place of Noah's Ark or the Holy Grail, so there's no point in arguing about it now. We just have to take our opinions with us.

In the main the new owners, to put it mildly, did not have a clue. In the main, the new owners, to be kind, were the last sort of people we wanted, lured by the sight of crowds packing Giants Stadium and believing that all they needed was franchise, a big stadium and some players and the way ahead would be golden. It didn't take too long to become tarnished. The new ones, like some of the old, simply could not handle defeat or lack of success off the field either. It wasn't their fault, could not possibly be their fault. Not their hired hands' fault, either, because they were chosen by the owner and he was very unlikely to have made a mistake in that direction, either. So if it wasn't his fault and it wasn't his chosen people's faults then it could only be the fault of . . . tah rah . . . the game itself. I think of it as the start of what became an American malaise in which the individual is never at fault, never responsible, it is the other person, the other thing, the other corporation; the coffee shop if the coffee is scalding hot and you're clumsy enough to spill it, the hamburger chain if you're gross enough to stuff down sacks full of Big Macs every day; the ladder if you slipped, the gun if you shot someone. Sad.

Owners through most of the time were a fairly conservative bunch. That changed. Rock stars, their agents and managers, middle-aged men with open shirts, hairy chests, dangling gold medallions and rings to match. Lamar Hunt, looking round the room, commenting drily: We have a different looking league. The carpetbaggers came from all over. They were the newly rich, in the main, looking at the wonderful times in New Jersey and looking at a boost to their already overblown egos. We would take anyone's money for a franchise; well, almost anyone. We did turn down the boxing promoter Don King. We should have turned down two groups from England, one led by Ralph Sweet, former vice chairman of the oldest pro club in the world, Notts County, who did their best to bring stilted English attitudes and ruin the Minnesota Kicks and Jimmy Hill, a noted, notorious (?) player, manager, union leader, TV pundit and all-round self-promoter who first took over Detroit, ruined that, and moved to Washington DC and ruined that.

Sweet, with problems mounting over the use of the new Metrodome, built to replace the ageing but highly successful Metropolitan Stadium— where the Kicks had averaged over 20,000 throughout the years—caught a plane back to England and told club chief Tommy Scallen over the phone that he wasn't putting any more money into it. Some of the newcomers came to less than satisfactory personal ends. Nelson Skalbania, a shaker and mover in Alberta, owner along the way of the hockey teams Edmonton Oilers, Indianapolis Racers (and Wayne Gretzky), Atlanta Flames and the CFL's Montreal Alouettes and BC Lions, ended up doing more jail time than his Calgary club spent in the league. Karsten von Wersebe was embroiled in a major fraud case involving the Rothschild Bank in Zurich, one of whose chief officers went on the run and was finally caught in Thailand. Sir Evelyn Rothschild blamed the troubles on $115 million of improper loans to von Wersebe and his associate in Canada and elsewhere Wolfgang Stolzenberg. I never did find out what happened to Karsten but, then, he was a quiet and distant man even when he was around.

Skalbania's Calgary came and went, in effect, in a puff of smoke. We were at the annual meeting at the end of their first and only season, when it came time for the vote to be taken to see who was going to post their bond and play the next year. With the vote being taken alphabetically, Skalbania of Calgary was early in the voting and Peter Pocklington, of Edmonton, was next in line and next to vote. Skalbania said "hold on a minute" and he and Pocklington began talking and scribbling on the back of a pack of cigarettes. We waited, bemused, until Skalbania announced that there was one yes vote for going forward; Calgary and Edmonton had just merged. Their deal was written on the cigarette packet. In the past, they had traded a hockey franchise for a diamond ring and some paintings, so this was just another part of the "aren't we clever, aren't we great guys"

clowning of the pair of them. Two great, clever guys who had once determined Gretzky's fate over a game of backgammon. All good, clean fun,
no doubt, if you don't give a damn, have more money than sense and have
no qualms about behaving irresponsibly to your partners, the game and
the public. If they had been around at the time, the scoundrels who ruined
Enron, WorldCom and Martha Stewart's pal at ImClone would have been
definite candidates for ownership. They would have fitted right in

This what the league looked like after the machinations of that winter
of 1977. Try to hold on to the facts, keep the pieces of the jigsaw in place
and don't lose your place: St Louis moved to Anaheim (they lasted three
more years), Team Hawaii caught a catamaran to Tulsa (bless them, they
were around for seven seasons), Las Vegas (there for one year only) went
to San Diego (for one more year only). Then in came Colorado (one year),
Detroit (three years, before moving to Washington for one year), Houston
Hurricanes and Memphis (for three years each), New England (three years
then to Jacksonville for two), Oakland (for one year), Philadelphia (for
three). Oh, and we lost Connecticut altogether.

No, it's not worth reading that again and trying to understand all that
went on. Just think how confusing, how crazy it must have seemed at the
time to the media, to the public . . . and to some of us. Behind it all was
another sign that we who had built the league this far were losing our grip.
The Executive Committee had always been elected league-wide, so that
those felt to be the best leaders would lead on behalf of all. Our gargantu-
an league of 24 teams was now broken into six divisions and at the first
possible league meeting, someone said the Executive Committee should
now consist of one representative from each division and there and then,
the divisions grouped in different parts of the room and picked their man.
The old Executive Committee was swept aside and with it the years of
experience and caring and mistakes-not-to-be-made again. I remember
turning to my neighbor and saying "there goes the league." The musical
chairs didn't end there, of course, this was simply the year of greatest
excess. Calgary came and went in one year, Atlanta in two, DC in one and
Team America, based in DC, also in one.

We also had a union to contend with a little later in the unstoppable
decline. John Kerr had been one of those busy players, buzzing round

midfield like a bee and buzzing round in later life like a b . . . (fill in your own letters) as the soccer person leading the charge to form a players' union, succeeding and causing immense problems in a league that was fragile enough already. I stress that John was the soccer person involved, because all the rest were from the NFL Players Association, lawyers from that other sport, funds from that other sport, attitude and inflexibility from that other sport. Obviously, nobody from that other sport gave a hoot about soccer or soccer players and either wanted to milk it or get rid of it. But why John Kerr allowed himself to be used, why he flung himself into the vanguard, when he must have known the damage he was inflicting is beyond me. All the owners were losing money, some a considerable amount, so many managers and coaches and PR people and marketers and sales people and secretaries were working as hard as people have ever worked, so many players were being decently treated and being paid a reasonable wage and yet along came people from another sport entirely, led by someone who had been one of our own, and created the kind of problems only sworn enemies could inflict. Lee Stern's opinion would get an answering nod from many: "That probably had more to do with the demise of the NASL than anything else. We spent so much time and so much money battling the union. The league wasn't ready for a union and if the NFL had had a union in the 1950s or early 1960s they would have never been able to get started."

Not everything went the union's way, of course, and Noel Lemon was certainly capable of finding ways to annoy them; annoy anyone, in fact, but in this case John Kerr:

"I was chairman of the competition committee at the time the union agreement called for Johnny Kerr, as union rep, to be on it, too. So I would have a little reception in my room the night before, and not invite him, and we'd agree on what we were going to do and then have the meeting with him present the next day and everything all wrapped up. I played against him when I first came over in '68 and battered him a few times. Then I didn't see him for a long while but as his son, who's a much nicer person than he is, was coming up into the draft I told John Kerr—I am going to draft him. Oh no, he says. Yes, I said, I'll draft him, sign him, put him in uniform and then just as he's going to run on the field for the first game, I'll tell him, bugger off, you're not playing. John Kerr says—I believe you would. And I said, no, not to your son, but I'd damn well do it to you if I had the chance."

Ted Howard, a much kinder, gentler person than Noel, is not without strong feelings, either:

> "I could never understand the venom he put into it. He had always been treated fairly, very fairly; almost all the players were being treated fairly. The only thing that needed to be put right was the matter of severance. Like anybody in this world, they could be fired if they were not good enough but they could be out of a job in a few days with no income— that needed correcting, but that's all. So we had a strike, lasted two or three weeks, clubs had to find replacement players from anywhere, I know Memphis signed some from the local amateur league. It was really bad, we spent so much time and money which would have been better spent in many other directions. The only funny thing in the whole affair happened at a meeting in DC. We went down, Phil and I and others, to meet with our lawyer Bob Rolnick and the union people, headed by Ed Garvey. Well, we talked and argued and then Bob Rolnick, who had no sense of humor at all, said to Garvey "can we go into your office, we need to cactus." "Cactus? said Garvey "you want to what? Cactus?" Yes, said Bob, that's when the pricks are on the outside."

Noel Lemon recalls that the strike was called for a Saturday night. "All the players were supposed to walk off the field right after the national anthem. Fort Lauderdale's players did that, I remember. We were playing Rochester in Tulsa and on the far side of the field I had two entire teams, one with our uniforms, one with Rochester's spare set, with their jackets on, covering the uniforms, ready to come on if they were needed. But they weren't."

Despite the abandonment of the Long Term Strategic Plan, abandoned in the snow without another thought, there was one more chance given of a firm future, through the mind and vision of Sonny Werblin. Plainly a man of great vision, Sonny Werblin was the owner of the New York Jets when he signed Joe Namath and turned the unsuccessful successors to the truly awful New York Titans into a modern phenomenon. He was also the driving force behind the Meadowlands, the site of the race track, the indoor arena and Giants Stadium (which is accomplishment enough) but he also, bless his heart, made sure the playing area was wide enough for soccer, not a traditional American Football field where you had to go up into row 6 of the stands to find any room to run up for a corner. Sixty yards, even 58 yards, was a width we often had to suffer in. Sonny made sure Giants Stadium was wide enough for the soccer boom he saw coming; wide enough for us and wide enough in 1994 for the World Cup.

But if that was vision, what came later tragically foresaw the end of the NASL; at a time, as I say, when externally there was much to brag about— the Cosmos filling the stadium and 30,000, 40,000 not uncommon from Vancouver and Seattle to Tampa Bay via Minnesota. In short, the glory days. Sonny was then head of Madison Square Garden and his group, by then, owned the Washington Diplomats and he and his chief executive Jack Krumpe turned up at an annual meeting of the League, at L'Enfant Plaza in DC, to make the Big Bang argument. Guys (and I paraphrase but this is the guts of us), we have some good clubs, well-financed and we have a bunch of weak sisters, ill-financed. We have to get rid of those and then we can go forward successfully, knowing we will succeed. That's the Big Bang, get rid of all the weak sisters at once, and we'll move our club to Shea Stadium, buying that territory from the Cosmos, and build a fantastic rivalry in a strongly financed League. If we do not do this now, then we will lose people bit by bit along the way . . . that's the Little Bang.

The support he gained was not enough; Warner Communications wanted $4 million for the territory east of the Hudson River, a ridiculous sum, and the Big Bang Theory began and ended with Sonny Werblin's words. The glory days rolled on but Sonny Werblin's Little Bang was off in the corner having its fuse fixed, ready to be lit.

Apart from opposing expansion, the Long Term Strategic Plan Committee had also opposed any network contract until we could all produce a reasonably filled stadium and thus convince TV viewers they were missing something. We lost that vote as well and ABC was on board, and shipping water fast, as Little Bangs sounded in the distance and ABC came to Canada. We were playing Los Angeles at Toronto's CNE Stadium, right on the shores of Lake Ontario, on a beautiful summer Sunday afternoon in a country where winter is long and harsh and the inhabitants take every opportunity to enjoy the weather when it comes. We had worked hard to get about 14,000 people into the stadium and packed them all on one side, so that the cameras would see a nice, healthy crowd and soccer fans tuning in all across the two nations would be impressed, or at least not depressed by what they saw. But ABC was already, plainly, showing their growing indifference and refused to spend a penny on building a small platform on the opposite side of the field, insisting on shooting from the same side as the crowd. Thus it was that ABC's audience that day saw a soccer match watched, on the far side, by some passing seagulls, who perched for a while and moved on, while over the top of the stadium could be seen the passing sails of Lake Ontario yachtsmen. Sails and seagulls, not to mention a terrible game on the hardest, worst artificial surface (except maybe Spartan Stadium, Philadelphia) in the entire league.

As Noel Lemon puts it: "We did an awful lot of things to hurt ourselves in the NASL. The ABC contract hurt us. We were so concerned with being on national TV but they put us on at 2 in the afternoon in the middle of summer. I was interested and involved in the league but I didn't watch because I was out on the course playing golf. We prostituted ourselves for a little money and when the ratings were low and they dropped us, that was another negative story . . . but people are going to look back years from now and see the NASL as just another steppingstone for soccer in this country." And Jack Krumpe, chief executive of Madison Square Garden, owner of the Diplomats, not, like us a soccer person but a first class executive, one of too few, concurred: "I think we sold our souls to national television and we've gotten very little in return."

Apart from our own self-inflicted wounds, one of the other sports that had no love for the NASL, came out of its shell and did great harm with, one is entitled to think, malice aforethought. The National Football League had been rolling merrily along for years, with its sold-out stadia and massive TV contracts, the very picture of a successful professional sports league with nary a chink in their armor and no opposition on the horizon and happy owners raking in the loot. Then, suddenly, they made a decision that their owners would indeed be their owners and the owners of nothing else in sport. And guess what other sport rejoiced in having NFL owners among their strongest and staunchest? Why, the NASL, in case you didn't guess, the NASL and Lamar Hunt and Joe Robbie. The NFL had never bothered before and never bothered since but they decided to do it when we looked, on the outside, as if success, guaranteed, overall success, was at our feet. Coincidence? Well, we sued them anyway and spent time and money on lawyers and depositions and finally giving what I thought was compelling evidence. It was certainly compelling enough for us to win the lawsuit and get the munificent sum of $1 in damages as well as repayment of our legal expenses. As Charles Dickens' Mr Bumble once remarked "the law, sir, is an ass, a idiot." Until that lawsuit, the firm for which Paul Tagliabue worked was also our law firm and Tagliabue, of course, later became Commissioner of the NFL.

There was still time for the bizarre and Ted Howard recalls a bit of British bizarre:

> "During all this, we went to Minnesota for a TV game and the Kicks' people were excited because Debbie Reynolds was in town and she had agreed to sing the national anthem. Next day they said we have bad news and we have good news . . . Debbie Reynolds has a cold and has called off but the lead singer of the English rock group Three Dog Night has agreed to sing. Well, thank god the TV was away for a commercial. The guy didn't know the tune, didn't know the words. It was unrecognisable, nobody has ever heard the national anthem sung that way. There was no music to help him or drown him out, just this voice and this hideous song he was singing."

And so we stumbled on, with fewer people taking fewer, halting steps until we came to the year George Orwell chose as the year for his bleak and bitter book on the future, with the good and the free fighting against all odds against a controlled media and an indoctrinated public.1984.

We didn't know it at the time, but the last NASL game was game 2 of what had now become the best-of-three championship series between an old club of mine, the Chicago Sting and my current club, the Toronto Blizzard at Varsity Stadium, no more alas, in downtown Toronto. We had lost in Chicago and we lost 3–2 at home and that was that. Consider it ironic or appropriate but Chicago's last two goals, the last two goals of the NASL, were shots deflected, massively deflected, one by Derek Spalding and one by Connie Karlsson, into the opposite side from where Paul Hammond was diving to save quite comfortably.

19

A (VERY) SHORT SPELL AT THE TOP

THE LAST THING I wanted to be was President of the NASL and that's what I was. President. The last. By the time I was coerced into that position the League was beyond saving; at least by me. Over the years, as owners will when they are momentarily unhappy with the incumbent, one or other had taken me to one side and asked me if I wanted to replace Phil Woosnam. I never wanted to and tried to make it clear.

I liked running a club, the competition, the cut and thrust, the surreptitious trips to far places to sign a player, the daily talk with the coach about the team, with the PR people on the tale we wanted to tell, with the marketing efforts, with the planning of development of players for the future, the satisfaction of seeing a team come together. If I had been a General, I'd rather have been a Patton than an Eisenhower, a Benedict Arnold at Saratoga rather than an Horatio Gates.

(And before anyone gets exercised at the mention of the eventual turncoat Arnold, let me tell them this little piece of history. At Saratoga Battlefield, down the corner on a slope, is a statue, a plinth, on which is carved the leg and boot of a cavalryman. No name, no identification but it the leg and boot of Benedict Arnold, gravely wounded on that spot while the overall Commander, Gates, sat in his tent. Arnold won that battle. If the musket ball which wounded his leg had been two feet higher, he'd have been killed and would now be placed on the highest level of the pantheon of American heroes. Instead, he lived and eventually became a traitor, reviled by one side and scorned by the other. Of such small moments and infinitesimal distances are all our fates determined, though few so drastically as Arnold's.)

But, back to my fate. The League called and I went. Howard Samuels had died on October 25, 1984 and the only cavalry to come riding to the rescue was me, then Chairman of the Board of the Toronto Blizzard, and appointed unanimously as interim CEO and League President, so the press release said, on December 12. Well, who else was there? And if I was the cavalry then it was soon clear that I was coming alone and the besieged were just about out of ammunition. Some of the ammunition needed was a belief by each and every owner that the rot could be stopped. It was not there. On the purely physical level, there was the document called a Performance Bond. Each year, the League set the amount of the bond and the date by which it had to be posted, ensuring that on that given day we all knew who was financially and legally committed to play the next season. No pay, no play, no more ownership. If you paid but then did not play, you lost the entire amount of the bond, then up into the hundreds of thousands, as well as your franchise. But Howard had played fast and loose with that vital piece of machinery. He had, for example, given Tampa Bay Rowdies several extra months to post theirs, to let them have a free look at what might happen and this, of course, meant that the others had no idea who their eventual partners might be.

Only two clubs, Joe Robbie's Minnesota and my own Toronto, had posted proper bonds when I first walked in as boss of the League to find, among other things, that we had as many lawyers as we had clubs. I did get a nice note from Lamar Hunt, headed "To The Last of the Great Survivors. Thinking back to the underground motel room in Chicago along about 1970, I somehow knew you'd be where you are! Seriously—congratulations on your new position and all good wishes for success." But Lamar, the ownership rock of early years, was already gone.

I was close to talking a banker in Charlotte into the fold and even closer to convincing Peter Kane, a Texas oil man from England, and devout Middlesbrough fan, but he had second, and in the end better, thoughts. Jack Warner, later to become FIFA Vice President and President of CONCACAF came up from Trinidad to suggest a Caribbean franchise, drawn from all the islands and playing home games in some of them and in Miami. At other times, it might have worked but not with so few bona fide clubs on the mainland. Still, there was hope and several others who might have said "yes" when I went one day to Vancouver and was in the middle of a meeting with a fine group of local people who were going to take over the Whitecaps when one of their group walked in with a wire service story—the Cosmos were not going to post their performance bond, said president Chinaglia. End of meeting. End of hope. Only Minnesota and Toronto were committed and while we had lived with five clubs in the past, two just wouldn't make it.

Formal and legal to the end, we followed the League Constitution and held a formal hearing at which the Cosmos were charged with failing to post a performance bond—a charge which, if proven, and that was simple enough, carried the penalty of expulsion from the League. Mark Beinstock, the League counsel, conducted the hearing, as he should, and I sat there, giving evidence, fully conscious of the irony. Here was this club that I had started 14 years before, before it was born, before it had a name, or a coach, or a stadium or player and here I was, being part of its death. President Chinaglia, whom I had blamed, and still blame, for many of the Cosmos' ills, had not, of course, posted his performance bond. But his performance was true to form. He threatened to throw Mark Beinstock out of the window. None of us worked out just how, and certainly not why, the Cosmos franchise was transferred from Warner Communications, a major public company, to Chinaglia. The League office had no documentation, the lawyers were in the dark, it just happened and remains murky to this day. In retrospect, it is obvious that no legal transfer ever took place and that it wasn't Giorgio we were drumming out of the league but Warner itself, which would have made a pretty story at the time.

Peppe Pinton, for some time an aide and comfort to Chinaglia and later his own man, eventually came into possession of the name and ran Cosmos Soccer Camps, protected the mountain of videos and other relics. "Giorgio never owned the Cosmos," he said. "It took me many years, bit by bit to get it from Warner. But the Cosmos are like Marilyn Monroe. Everyone remembers." Chinaglia, of course, also took over Lazio, one of the two Serie A clubs of Rome, mostly, if not entirely, with finance raised in the NY/NJ area, and practically ruined that club, too. Not bad going, to ruin two famous clubs in one year.

My thoughts and feelings about those late and declining days have changed not at all in the intervening years. That became crystal clear when I started to preach on this topic and the thought struck me that I'd seen these words before, maybe even said them, so I sorted through the files and closets in the basement and, lo and behold, found an article, two in fact, almost identical, written by the late Dan Herbst. I can not say it better than Dan quoted me long years ago:

"We have not been able to tell people since 1977–78 that this is what we stand for. . . . What we lacked was consistency, stability and continuity. Every year we had a different crusade that was going to be the panacea for all our ills. Anyone who is not optimistic about the future of soccer in America must be blind, deaf and dumb and stupid to boot. The fact is, the game is blossoming at every conceivable level except ours. In 1969, a deliberate policy decision was made that we would be an integral part of the building of the game. Our clubs spent as much time in propagating the word as in running their own operations. Since 1979 we have become apart from the game. This league, at the club level, has by and large, disassociated itself from its soccer community. Many franchises that started in later years would not listen to those of us who had built clubs in a community way. They felt they needed to do nothing more than rent a stadium, spend so much money on players and, eureka!—success was going to be at their doorstep.

At the league level there was great antagonism towards the USSF and CSA and a total disinterest in helping the national team programs. We made a series of enormously erratic decisions. We made indoor soccer participation mandatory. Then we made it voluntary and then we made it mandatory again. In one season, we changed our playing rules three times, on one occasion not making a decision on what rules we'd play under until the opening day of the season. I remember sitting in an hotel room in Jacksonville as we were about to play a match and having a league-wide conference call to determine whether we were going to use the 35-yard line. I then had to run down and tell my coach: "This is what we're going to do today." Then we changed it and changed it back again. We allowed franchises to pick up and move at will. We permitted those dreadful owners in Detroit to move to Washington, thereby allowing them to ruin two cities, instead of just the one they had already ruined."

There are those, said Dan, who argue that the signing of Pele did more harm than good. Well, tell that to the Marines, say I. The huge Cosmos crowds wouldn't have hurt us if we'd learned the right lessons from them. We drew 77,000 people not because we suddenly had a super stadium, Pele and Beckenbauer but because six years of bloody hard labor had created the stage where the Peles and Beckenbauers could perform. The signing of Pele became a double-edged sword because of the lack of understanding as to the reason for it and the reason for signing Beckenbauer. It was my firm intention that Franz would represent the last major expenditure that the Cosmos should make.

Getting Pele lifted us through a crust of indifference to where we could talk proudly about the other good things that were happening, and be listened to. We acquired Beckenbauer so nobody could say "What's going to happen after Pele goes?" I wanted to build the team around Franz and combine him with some good journeymen and young Americans. The maestro was good enough to handle a team in which five young players were learning their trade. Unfortunately, after I left the Cosmos, the reverse took place and zillions were spent on so and so and so on and on; so many great players, so many not needed. A guy called from a Dallas radio station one day to ask where we'd gone wrong. I said to him—"If one week you're a country and western station, the next week you're a rock 'n roll station, the next classical and the following an all-news station, you will soon lose all of your listeners. In essence, we've done the same thing within our league."

Finally, Dan had raised the issue of the endless tinkering with the game "by upstart owners" to make it "more entertaining." My response then, as now, was, or is: "If you want entertainment, go to the ballet. Sports isn't about entertainment, it's about passion. If you are completely neutral, I defy you to enjoy any sporting event because there is absolutely nothing inherently entertaining in sports. If you take away spectators and their noise and a game's meaning (to them), there is nothing left." I should have said it to Carl Berg in San Jose that night in 1983, the man who once remarked that I must go to bed with a FIFA Handbook beside my bed instead of a bible. Not that I didn't say this, or a reasonable facsimile thereof, enough times to enough people, mostly to those who didn't listen or who thought I was an idiot. Well, maybe I was. But it is what I believe.

So, the NASL's rights and assets, including the considerable sums paid back from those incredible legal costs from the lawsuit against the NFL, went into what the lawyer's call a liquidating trust, in the hands, of course, of a lawyer and we closed the door and left. There was a note in the New York *Times,* buried under Transactions, an Etc, that the NASL had disbanded. Vince Casey, one time New England Tea Men and League PR man, talked about it. "Five, six years after we hit the heights and all we get is a line in the Etcetera column. I think back to the glory days. My two greatest thrills in this business were the FIFA World All Star Game in 1982, when 77,000 people stood up and sang the National Anthem at

Giants Stadium and when the Tea Men beat the Cosmos, before a crowd of 62,498 in 1978. It's incredible to imagine that five or six years later, we're just an etcetera."

I have no precise memories of that day; the League and the League office were, to me, not personal; not in the same way that telling the Blizzard staff and players that the end had come. That was very personal for me; for some of the older players it was just another contract come to an end but for the great crop of young Canadian players we had assembled—Pasquale de Luca, Trevor McCallum, Randy Ragan, Charlie Falzon, Paul James, Lyndon Hooper and others—it was an end to their full professional careers almost before they had begun. Dale Barnes painted the bleakest picture "When the Blizzard died, that was really the end of professional soccer in Canada." Paul James spoke later for the young players: "We didn't realize at the time how bad it was; didn't realize all clubs were not like the Blizzard. What a difference. We still talk about it." Coach Bob Houghton looked upon it as a job half done: "We worked very hard the last three years to challenge Canadian players to prove they could be world class. They proved it and now there is nowhere for them to play." There was, in fact, one place remaining . . . the World Cup. With a backbone of former NASL players, Canada qualified for its only World Cup finals in 1986, a point so well made by Canada's Bruce Wilson, the left back for Vancouver, Cosmos and twice for me at Chicago and Toronto, in 2003 when he was inducted into the US Soccer Hall of Fame.

So how do I end this, with mostly fond memories, warmth and respect for a lot of good people and not another thought to be given to the other kind? Perhaps by borrowing a couple of lines from Henry V's speech on St. Crispins Day, the night before the battle of Agincourt when we annihilated the French: We few, we happy few, we band of brothers.

Or perhaps by taking the first, great line from Martin Luther King: I have a dream. Or my own closing words at my own induction into the Hall of Fame: ". . . a great game, great people, great clubs, a great league." Indeed it was, never to be repeated. But, no, in the end I think it'll be that old Scottish soldiers' toast, preferably with a glass of Laphroig or Macallan or somesuch in hand. So, ready then lads? Here's Tae Us—Wha's Like Us?—Damn Few.

20

LIFE AFTER . . .

SO, WHAT DO you do when your entire industry disappears not over time but overnight? Some NASL people floated back overseas, some remain today coaching kids or working at the game in places all over the USA. Some went into major league baseball, the NBA, even the NFL, poor souls. I went into soccer and found the one person willing to hire me. Me. And my employer allowed me to delve into such actions as promoting major tournaments from Miami to New York to Los Angeles, Beijing and Tokyo . . . and being one of the founders of the American Professional Soccer League (along with Chuck Blazer), one of the small leagues which over time blended into today's United Soccer Leagues.

Then there was The Day The World Played Football; to celebrate the 50th anniversary of the founding of the United Nations. We had 128 countries taking part in a rolling schedule across all the time zones of the world with a ball carried in the Mir spaceship for good measure.

That was when I was on speaking terms with FIFA but later, in turning the incredible collection of art and memorabilia, put together by Harry Langton, into the FIFA Museum Collection, my little band of four people fell foul of the mighty lords of world football and ended up being sued and, in turn, suing back. Both lawsuits were under Swiss law in Swiss courts. We won both of the lawsuits and that is akin to winning the seventh game of the World Series at Yankee Stadium when the umpires are all relatives of George Steinbrenner, so you can judge for yourselves how valid were our positions and actions. Pity the same can not be said for the governing body of world football. Despite that, I have been Senior Consultant to CONCACAF since 1998 and was President of the New York Committee for the World Cup of 1994 which gave me the chance to relay one of the greatest tales of all time.

I was called in for the task late because, as we know, the World Cup was to be played across the Hudson in New Jersey and all the Jersey folks were making a meal out of it without throwing even a bone back across the river to New York. So my task was to plan some events, make some noise, do whatever could be done, wherever it could be done . . . and obvious locations were the parks of New York City, especially Central Park. A meeting was thus arranged with the top brass of the City of New York Parks Department and along I went to meet the number two person, a very serious lady who listened to what I wanted and then said: What were those dates you gave me? So I told her the dates of the World Cup, the biggest sporting event on the globe with billions around the world waiting spellbound for it. I'm sorry, she said, in sepulchural tones, but you'll have to change the dates . . . that is the week of the Gay Games and we're busy. Pause. Rewind. You'll have to change the dates of the World Cup . . . never mind why or what else was going on. How blind, how totally out of touch with the world can anyone be?

Apart from being coerced back into coaching kids, the Ossining Storm, that's about it. But I really will have to decide soon what I'm going to do when I grow up.

APPENDIX

1967

NPSL

Atlanta Chiefs	Baltimore Bays
New York Generals	Chicago Spurs (to Kansas City)
Philadelphia Spartans (D)	Pittsburgh Phantoms (D)
Oakland Clippers	Toronto Falcons
St. Louis Stars	Los Angeles Toros (to San Diego)

USA

Boston Rovers (D)	Chicago Mustangs
Cleveland Stokers	New York Skyliners (D)
Dallas Tornado	Houston Stars
Detroit Cougars	Toronto City (D)
Los Angeles Wolves	Vancouver Canadians (D)
San Francisco Gales (D)	Washington Whips

1968

Atlanta Chiefs	Kansas City Spurs	San Diego Toros (D)	Detroit Cougars (D)	Houston Stars (D)
Baltimore Bays	Boston Beacons (D)	Chicago Mustangs (D)	Los Angeles Wolves (D)	New York Generals (D)
Cleveland Stokers (D)	Dallas Tornado		Oakland Clippers (D)	St. Louis Stars
Toronto Falcons (D)	Vancouver Royals (D)		Washington Whips (D)	

1969

Atlanta Chiefs	Baltimore Bays (D)
Dallas Tornado	Kansas City Spurs
	St. Louis Stars

1970

Atlanta Chiefs	Dallas Tornado
Kansas City Spurs (D)	Rochester Lancers
St. Louis Stars	Washington Darts

1971

Atlanta Chiefs	Dallas Tornado	St. Louis Stars
Montreal Olympique	New York Cosmos	Washington Darts (to Miami Gatos)
Toronto Metros	Rochester Lancers	

1972

Atlanta Chiefs	Dallas Tornado	St. Louis Stars
Montreal Olympique	New York Cosmos	Miami Gatos
Toronto Metros	Rochester Lancers	

1973

Atlanta Chiefs became Apollos (D)	Dallas Tornado	St. Louis Stars
Montreal Olympique (D)	New York Cosmos	Miami Gatos (to Miami Toros)
Toronto Metros	Rochester Lancers	Philadelphia Atoms

1974

Baltimore Comets	Dallas Tornado	Miami Toros
Boston Minutemen	Denver Dynamo	Philadelphia Atoms
Rochester Lancers	Toronto Metros	New York Cosmos
Washington Diplomats	St. Louis Stars	Los Angeles Aztecs
San Jose Earthquakes	Seattle Sounders	Vancouver Whitecaps

1975

Baltimore Comets (to San Diego Jaws)	Dallas Tornado	Miami Toros
Boston Minutemen	Denver Dynamo (D)	Philadelphia Atoms
Rochester Lancers	Toronto Metros became Metros-Croatia	New York Cosmos
Washington Diplomats	St. Louis Stars	Los Angeles Aztecs
San Jose Earthquakes	Seattle Sounders	Vancouver Whitecaps
Chicago Sting	Hartford Bi-Centennials	Portland Timbers
San Antonio Thunder	Tampa Bay Rowdies	

1976

Boston Minutemen (D)	Dallas Tornado	Miami Toros (to Ft. Lauderdale Strikers)
Rochester Lancers	Toronto Metros-Croatia	Philadelphia Atoms (D)
Washington Diplomats	St. Louis Stars	New York Cosmos
San Jose Earthquakes	Seattle Sounders	Los Angeles Aztecs
Chicago Sting	Hartford Bi-Centennials (to New Haven)	Vancouver Whitecaps
San Antonio Thunder (to Team Hawaii)	Tampa Bay Rowdies	Portland Timbers
San Diego Jaws (to Las Vegas Quicksilver)		Minnesota Kicks

1977

Chicago Sting (to Oakland Stompers)	Connecticut Bi-Centennials	Ft. Lauderdale Strikers
Dallas Tornado	Team Hawaii (to Tulsa Roughnecks))	Rochester Lancers
Toronto Metros-Croatia	St. Louis Stars (to California Surf)	Washington Diplomats
New York Cosmos	Tampa Bay Rowdies	Seattle Sounders
Minnesota Kicks	Vancouver Whitecaps	San Jose Earthquakes
Portland Timbers	Los Angeles Aztecs	Las Vegas Quicksilver (to San Diego Sockers)

1978

Chicago Sting	California Surf	Ft. Lauderdale Strikers
Dallas Tornado	Tampa Bay Rowdies	Rochester Lancers
Toronto Metros-Croatia	Vancouver Whitecaps	Washington Diplomats
New York Cosmos	Los Angeles Aztecs	Seattle Sounders
Minnesota Kicks	Colorado Caribous (to Atlanta Chiefs)	San Jose Earthquakes
Portland Timbers	Memphis Rogues	Detroit Express
Houston Hurricane	Philadelphia Fury	New England Tea Men
Oakland Stompers (to Edmonton Drillers)	Tulsa Roughnecks	San Diego Sockers

1979

Chicago Sting	Tampa Bay Rowdies	Ft. Lauderdale Strikers
Dallas Tornado	Vancouver Whitecaps	Rochester Lancers
Toronto Metros-Croatia (to Toronto Blizzard)	Los Angeles Aztecs	Washington Diplomats
New York Cosmos	Memphis Rogues	Seattle Sounders
Minnesota Kicks	Philadelphia Fury	San Jose Earthquakes
Portland Timbers	Edmonton Drillers	Detroit Express
California Surf	Tulsa Roughnecks	New England Tea Men
Houston Hurricane	Atlanta Chiefs	San Diego Sockers

1980

Chicago Sting	Tampa Bay Rowdies	Ft. Lauderdale Strikers)
Dallas Tornado	Vancouver Whitecaps	Rochester Lancers (D)
Toronto Blizzard	Los Angeles Aztecs	Washington Diplomats
New York Cosmos	Memphis Rogues (D)	Seattle Sounders
Minnesota Kicks	Philadelphia Fury) (to Montreal Manic	San Jose Earthquakes
Portland Timbers	Edmonton Drillers	Detroit Express (D)
California Surf		New England Tea Men (to Jacksonville Tea Men)
Houston Hurricane (D)	Tulsa Roughnecks	San Diego Sockers Atlanta Chiefs

1981

Chicago Sting	Ft. Lauderdale Strikers
Dallas Tornado (D)	Washington Diplomats (D)
Toronto Blizzard	Seattle Sounders
New York Cosmos	San Jose Earthquakes
Minnesota Kicks (D)	San Diego Sockers
Portland Timbers	Calgary Boomers (D)
California Surf (D)	Jacksonville Teamen
Tampa Bay Rowdies	
Vancouver Whitecaps	
Los Angeles Aztecs (D)	
Edmonton Drillers (T13	
Atlanta Chiefs (D)	
Tulsa Roughnecks	
Montreal Manic	

1982

Chicago Sting	Ft. Lauderdale Strikers
Toronto Blizzard	Seattle Sounders
New York Cosmos	San Jose Earthquakes
Portland Timbers (D)	San Diego Sockers
	Jacksonville Tea Men (D)
Tampa Bay Rowdies	
Vancouver Whitecaps	
Edmonton Drillers (D)	
Tulsa Roughnecks	
Montreal Manic	

1983

Chicago Sting	Tampa Bay Rowdies	Ft. Lauderdale Strikers (to Minnesota Strikers)
Toronto Blizzard	Vancouver Whitecaps	Seattle Sounders (D)
New York Cosmos		San Jose (to Golden Bay Earthquakes)
Tulsa Roughnecks		San Diego Sockers
Team America (D)		Montreal Manic (D)

1984

Chicago Sting (D)	Tampa Bay Rowdies (D)	Golden Bay Earthquakes (D)
Toronto Blizzard	Vancouver Whitecaps (D)	San Diego Sockers (D)
New York Cosmos (D)	Tulsa Roughnecks (D)	Minnesota Strikers

1985

Toronto Blizzard (D)	Minnesota Strikers (D)

R.I.P.

INDEX